Past Masters
General Editor    Keith Thomas

# Plato

R. M. Hare is White's Professor Emeritus of Moral Philosophy at Oxford University, Fellow of Corpus Christi College, and Professor of Philosophy Emeritus at the University of Florida. His other books include *The Language of Morals*, *Freedom and Reason*, and *Moral Thinking*, all published by Oxford University Press.

D0933132

# Past Masters

AQUINAS  Anthony Kenny
ARISTOTLE  Jonathan Barnes
AUGUSTINE  Henry Chadwick
BENTHAM  John Dinwiddy
THE BUDDHA  Michael Carrithers
CLAUSEWITZ  Michael Howard
COLERIDGE  Richard Holmes
DARWIN  Jonathan Howard
DESCARTES  Tom Sorell
DISRAELI  John Vincent
DURKHEIM  Frank Parkin
GEORGE ELIOT  Rosemary Ashton
ENGELS  Terrell Carver
ERASMUS  James McConica
FREUD  Anthony Storr
GALILEO  Stillman Drake
GOETHE  T. J. Reed
HEGEL  Peter Singer
HOBBES  Richard Tuck
HOMER  Jasper Griffin
HUME  A. J. Ayer
JESUS  Humphrey Carpenter
JOHNSON  Pat Rogers
JUNG  Anthony Stevens
KANT  Roger Scruton
KEYNES  Robert Skidelsky
KIERKEGAARD  Patrick Gardiner

LEIBNIZ  G. MacDonald Ross
LOCKE  John Dunn
MACHIAVELLI  Quentin Skinner
MALTHUS  Donald Winch
MARX  Peter Singer
MONTAIGNE  Peter Burke
MONTESQUIEU  Judith N. Shklar
THOMAS MORE  Anthony Kenny
MUHAMMAD  Michael Cook
NEWMAN  Owen Chadwick
NIETZSCHE  Michael Tanner
PAINE  Mark Philp
PAUL  E. P. Sanders
PLATO  R. M. Hare
ROUSSEAU  Robert Wokler
RUSSELL  A. C. Grayling
SCHILLER  T. J. Reed
SCHOPENHAUER  Christopher
  Janaway
SHAKESPEARE  Germaine Greer
ADAM SMITH  D. D. Raphael
SPINOZA  Roger Scruton
TOCQUEVILLE  Larry Siedentop
VICO  Peter Burke
VIRGIL  Jasper Griffin
WITTGENSTEIN  A. C. Grayling

## Forthcoming

JOSEPH BUTLER  R. G. Frey
COPERNICUS  Owen Gingerich
GANDHI  Bhikhu Parekh
HEIDEGGER  Michael Inwood

SOCRATES  C. C. W. Taylor
WEBER  Peter Ghosh
and others

13.95

R. M. Hare

# Plato

Oxford   New York

OXFORD UNIVERSITY PRESS

COMMUNITY COLLEGE
LIBRARY

Oxford University Press, Walton Street, Oxford OX2 6DP

Oxford New York
Athens Auckland Bangkok Bombay
Calcutta Cape Town Dar es Salaam Delhi
Florence Hong Kong Istanbul Karachi
Kuala Lumpur Madras Madrid Melbourne
Mexico City Nairobi Paris Singapore
Taipei Tokyo Toronto

and associated companies in
Berlin Ibadan

Oxford is a trade mark of Oxford University Press

First published 1982 as an Oxford University Press paperback
Reissued 1996

British Library Cataloguing in Publication Data
Data available

ISBN 0-19-287585-X

20  19  18  17  16  15  14  13  12

Printed in Great Britain by
Biddles Ltd
Guildford and King's Lynn

# Preface

This book is not intended as an addition to the already enormous and growing literature of Platonic scholarship, but as an encouragement and help to ordinary people who wish to make Plato's acquaintance. For this reason I have on the whole concentrated on the easier, which means the earlier and middle, dialogues, though the later ones are not entirely neglected. It is safe to say that no single statement can be made in interpretation of Plato which some scholars will not dispute. I have tried to bring out what I think he is up to, in a way that will be comprehensible; but the limits of a popular book do not allow me to defend my views beyond giving a few references to the text. I do not think that they are all that unorthodox, and where there is a lot of dispute I have tried not to conceal it. Above all, I have aimed to show how relevant Plato's dialogues are to questions which trouble us, or should trouble us, today, including some very practical issues about education and politics. To bring this out I have occasionally mentioned the names of thinkers of the modern period; but nothing of importance in my account of Plato will be missed by a reader to whom these names mean nothing.

In concentrating on what I think is the nucleus of Plato's philosophy, I have had to neglect many interesting and important topics. I should have liked in particular to say more on his views about love and about the arts. I have not thought it necessary to dwell on the superb quality of his dialogues as literature and drama; they are still as fresh and delightful as ever, and need no salesman.

A number of colleagues have been kind enough at my request to look at and criticise my typescript, among them Sir Kenneth Dover, Professors Ackrill and Moravcsik, Jonathan Barnes, Russell Meiggs, Christopher Taylor and Julius Tomin. Although all of these know incomparably more about Plato than I do, I have been stubborn enough not always to agree with them; but all the same my debt to them is very great. I should never have undertaken, let alone completed, this book if I had not been privileged to spend the whole of 1980 at the Center for Advanced Study in the Behavioral Sciences at Stanford, where I was made so happy and free from worries that this and another larger book flowed from my typewriter without any of the usual interruptions and frustrations. I am enormously grateful to the Director and staff at the Center, and to Oxford University for letting me go there.

To avoid footnotes, the few references have been consigned to the end of the book, except for those to Plato, which are in brackets in the text, giving the pages of Stephanus' edition as used in the margin of nearly all modern editions and translations. References in brackets preceded by 'p.' are to pages in this book. In the very few Greek words I had to quote, and in proper names in the Index, I have indicated the quantity of vowels by putting a bar over all the long ones, and have used a system of transliteration which relates the Greek words closely to modern English words derived from them (for example, '*psȳchē*').

R. M. HARE

# Contents

# 1 Life and times

Although this is not a work of biography, it is necessary to say something about the environment in which Plato grew up; for without some grasp of this, we cannot understand how he became a philosopher, and became the kind of philosopher that he was. Of the biographical information that has survived much is unreliable, and very little is of relevance to his philosophical development. There are some letters ascribed to him, some of them explicitly autobiographical. Their genuineness is disputed; but even if spurious they are probably close enough in time to their subject to be of use as evidence. The anecdotes of later writers are mostly either doubtful or trivial or both. So we do not need to go into the question of whether, for example, having been named by his parents Aristocles, he got called Platon because of his broad shoulders or his broad forehead, and other such details. But we do know about at least three episodes in his life which must have made a profound impression on him, and which place him in his historical setting.

Plato was born in 427 BC into an upper class Athenian family, and lived to be eighty. He would have been old enough to witness with young and impressionable eyes the last scenes of a tragedy, the decline and fall of the Athenian Empire. And he lived long enough to see the first beginnings of an empire of a very different sort, that of Philip of Macedon, whose son Alexander conquered a large part of the known world. The intervening period was one of constant and inconclusive warfare between the little Greek city states, with first one and then another achieving a brief hegemony, but none managing to bring any unity to Greece. That was left to the Macedonians after Plato's day.

The Athenian Empire started with a moral basis as a league to secure the freedom of the Greek cities, after their wonderful victories which had delivered them from the threat of conquest by Persia at the beginning of the fifth century. Thucydides, whose history of the period should be read by anybody who wants to understand Plato, puts into the mouth of Pericles, the chief architect of the Empire, a speech in honour of the Athenians who had died in the war with Sparta; and it has become famous as an expression of the ideals which excited Athens in the generation before Plato. Plato parodies this speech in his *Menexenus*. The ideals are high, but not exclusively moral according to our way of thinking. Naked imperialism plays a large part in them, and Pericles is more concerned with the fine figure that Athens is cutting than with justice to the allies whom she was turning into subjects. She ruled them in an ever more grasping and tyrannical fashion, and used their tribute to build the temples on the Acropolis which still amaze us, as well as for the navy which was the basis of her power. Recalcitrant cities were punished with increasing severity as the fear of successful rebellion began to bite: Mytilene was threatened with massacre but reprieved at the eleventh hour; Melos actually suffered total extinction.

Reading dialogues like the *Gorgias* with the history of the Athenian Empire in mind, we can see that Plato was reacting with moral revulsion to an attitude of mind current in Greece at the national as well as the personal level: an attitude which valued honour and glory above the virtues which enable people to 'dwell together in unity'. Of the founders of the Empire he says 'Not moderation and uprightness, but harbours, and dockyards, and walls, and tribute-money, and such nonsense, were what they filled the city with' (519a).

For nearly all the last third of the fifth century, until her defeat in 405 BC, Athens was almost constantly at war with Sparta, which with her allies resisted and in the end brought down the Athenian power. Plato was old enough to have fought in the last part of the war, as all citizens were required to, but we have no reliable record of his military service. A man of his class would naturally have served in the cavalry; and his brothers are said in the *Republic* to have fought well (368a).

The mention of Plato's social position may remind us that there was another dimension to the struggles of the Greek cities during this and the next century. The warfare was not merely between but within the cities. Almost every city was divided politically between the upper class and the rest of the free citizens (the numerous slaves can be left out of this political reckoning). This must not be taken as implying that there were no well-born democrats; indeed patrician

Whigs like Pericles played the greatest part in the development of the democracy, and while it prospered, the imperial ideal enjoyed general support from all classes. But increasingly these well-born leaders gave place to self-made men of the people and their sons, who could make themselves congenial to the mass meeting which was their parliament. Plato's class looked on these demagogues with contempt, tinged with fear. The political feelings amid which he would have grown up are those expressed at the beginning of a political pamphlet of the day, the so-called *Polity of the Athenians*: 'The kind of polity the Athenians have chosen is one I do not commend; for by choosing it they have chosen that bad men should come off better than good men.'

Sparta, Athens' enemy, was from inclination and self-interest a supporter of aristocracy or oligarchy; the populist Athenian leaders were always the most violent advocates of the war against her, and the rich, whose wealth and way of life were at risk, showed less enthusiasm for it, as for the Empire. The ambitions that turned young upper-class Englishmen and other Europeans into imperialists in the nineteenth century were indeed there but the prospects were far less attractive; and so, contrary to our way of thinking, it was the poor who were the main beneficiaries and supporters of empire. In most cities the democrats favoured alliance with, or submission to, Athens, and the 'few' sought the support of Sparta.

As the war went on, the internal divisions in the cities became more bitter and more savage; and even after the defeat of Athens the same sort of thing went on throughout the fourth century. Unrestrained personal ambition was a main motive in politicians. In the *Meno* that not untypical young man, asked by Socrates to define 'virtue' or 'excellence', answers that the excellence of a *man* is to be able, while engaging in politics, to do good to one's friends and harm to one's enemies, while taking care not to come to any harm oneself (71e). And in the *Gorgias* another young man holds out as an object of envy Archelaus of Macedon, who by a series of murders of his nearest relatives made himself king (471b).

Athens herself was relatively free of the political murders and massacres which happened elsewhere in Greece; but all the same, if we were to read of events in fifth- and fourth-century Greece in a modern newspaper, we should be glad we did not live there, especially if we had not heard about its cultural achievements – did not know, for example, that the Parthenon was built during this time, or that year by year some of the world's greatest poets and dramatists were bringing out their plays in the festivals. We may note in passing that two moderately sanguinary political leaders, Critias, Plato's cousin, and Dionysius I of Syracuse (both of whom will feature in our story shortly), wrote tragedies which were performed in the Athenian competitions.

Of these two evils in Greece, strife between and strife within cities, Plato says little by way of a remedy for the former (on which his literary rival Isocrates has a better record), and in the *Laws* and elsewhere treats the latter as the principal problem needing solution (628a, b). He thought that civil strife could be ended by a good system of government, and to describe and justify such a system was one of his main aims.

Another more general cause contributed to the moral unsettlement of the Greek cities. This was their increasing intellectual sophistication, the effect, perhaps, of widening cultural horizons. There is a story told in Herodotus' history of the Persian Wars: a Persian ruler confronted some Greeks, who by custom burnt their dead relations, with some Indians, whose practice was to eat them, and concluded from the shocked reactions of both to the others' ways that

> Custom, the king of all,
> Gods and men alike,
> Is their guide.

Plato quotes the same lines of Pindar in the *Gorgias* (484b); they go on

> It justifies the greatest violence;
> Its hand is over all.

The word translated 'custom' also meant 'law'. We can see how the idea got around that law and morality were alike based on mere convention. There was not even a stable religious backing for them. Plato points out in the *Euthyphro* that the gods themselves are, according to tradition, at variance with one another; in heaven as on earth moral differences lead to civil war (7e).

Protagoras, who with Socrates was one of the great thinkers of the preceding generation, articulated this relativism in his doctrine that 'A man is a measure of all things: of what is, that it is, and of what is not, that it is not.' As Plato implies in the *Theaetetus* (152a), where he discusses the doctrine, Protagoras meant 'each man for himself'. We shall come back later to Socrates' and Plato's attempted rebuttal of this relativist view; but it is easy to see how the old moral restraints slipped away, especially in politics.

These factors – unscrupulous political strife and the growth of moral relativism – reinforced each other. Thucydides, in a philosophically penetrating passage, points out that it affected even the language in which thinking had to be done. In his discussion of the effects of political violence he says 'In justifying their actions, they reversed the customary descriptive meanings of words.' He gives examples: what would have been called 'an irresponsible gamble' got to be called 'a brave and comradely venture'. This process, referred to in similar terms in the *Republic* (560d), is the same as that which in recent times has been called 'persuasive definition'. Its immediate result was to turn morality upside down; but indirectly it had the effect of stimulating Socrates and Plato to look instead for a way of finding *secure* definitions of moral words or of the things they connote. That is why we find them asking 'What then *is* courage?'; 'What *is* uprightness?', and in general 'What *is* goodness?'

It is easy to imagine the young Plato, under the influence of Socrates, being inspired by the hope of answering such questions; but in other respects he grew up in an atmosphere of disillusion culminating in disaster. Its effect on him will have been heightened by his upper-class upbringing. As we have seen, the Athenian aristocrats were by no means wholehearted supporters of the Empire; most of them admired Sparta for its orderly and stable system of government, on which Plato's political ideas are in part modelled; and there was at least a suspicion that treachery by members of this class had contributed to the final naval disaster for Athens at Aegospotami.

At any rate when Sparta came to settle the affairs of defeated Athens, although she did not, as some had expected, massacre the democrats, she secured her own interest by installing an oligarchic government, called by its enemies 'The Thirty Tyrants', among whom were two relatives of Plato's: Critias, his mother's first cousin, and Charmides, his maternal uncle. Both receive friendly treatment in his dialogues. The Thirty were indeed tyrannical and arbitrary: Plato records, in the *Apology* (32c), Socrates' courageous refusal to arrest a fellow-citizen, the democrat Leon, whom they had selected for judicial murder. Their government did not last long; it was ousted by a democratic regime, whose record was more moderate. Athens had lost her former glory; she did not, however, sink into complete ignominy, but took her share in the ups and downs of Greek mini-power politics.

We may conceive what effect these events – the collapse of a no longer inspiring imperialist democracy followed by the wretched performance of the opposing party – had on the young Plato. An able man of his class would naturally have sought a place in public life, and there is evidence that he started with this ambition; but since the chief qualification for success in politics was a total lack of scruple, it is not surprising that he was frightened off. He is said to have written poetry when young, and from the evidence of his writings (including a few poems) he would have made a good poet; but he came to see that there was another more lasting way of affecting men's minds, and thus, he hoped, the course of events. Socrates is expressing Plato's own attitude to politics when he says in the *Republic*, 'It would be like a man among wild animals, not willing to join in their crimes, nor able by himself to resist the savagery of all the rest; before he could help the city or his friends he would come to a sticky end without doing any good for himself or anybody else' (496d).

In 399 BC, after the restoration of the democracy, Socrates, Plato's idol, was tried on a charge of disbelief in the gods and corrupting the young, and condemned to death. The effect on Plato was profound and several of his dialogues are related to this event: Socrates' *Apology* or defence at his trial; the *Crito* in which he gives reasons for not making his escape after his condemnation, which would have been easy; and the *Phaedo*, in which he spends his last hours arguing for the immortality of the soul; and there are a number of smaller allusions. Plato seems to have resolved to devote his life to the exposition and development of Socrates' ideas.

Plato's distaste for political action can only have been strengthened by the outcome of his only active intervention in politics.

This occurred not in his own city of Athens but at Syracuse in Sicily, at the court of Dionysius I, and of his son and namesake. We do not know why Plato first went to Sicily, when he was about forty; but it may have been as an offshoot of a purely philosophical visit to the neighbouring Italian cities, which boasted some distinguished philosophers, especially the followers of Pythagoras. When he was in Syracuse he formed a deep personal affection for the young Dion, whose sister was married to Dionysius I, and who himself married his own niece, her daughter. Plato later wrote a poem on Dion in which he called the relation 'love', and said that it had driven him out of his mind. According to Greek ideas there was nothing unusual about this, and the second remark seems no great exaggeration if we think of the things that Dion later persuaded Plato to do, against his own better judgement.

Dion became Plato's pupil and absorbed his doctrine. We do not know how long Plato's first visit to Sicily lasted. There is an improbable story that Dionysius caused him to be sold into slavery, whence he was ransomed by friends. He returned to Athens, and there founded a philosophical school called, from its location in the grove dedicated to the hero Academus, the Academy. In it Plato and his fellow-philosophers shared a common table and engaged in mathematics, dialectic (that is, philosophy) and other studies, all seen as relevant to the training of statesmen. It was not the first such institution, but was probably modelled on similar communities of the Pythagoreans in Italy. Aristotle was only one of its distinguished members, and it lasted for centuries.

When Plato was about sixty, Dionysius I died and was succeeded by his son Dionysius II, whose uncle Dion conceived the idea that the young ruler might be moulded by Plato into the philosopher-king of the *Republic*. This was an unpromising scheme from the beginning, and it is likely that Plato accepted the invitation to Syracuse with reluctance and few hopes. But it was hard for him to resist the challenge, in view of what he had said in the *Republic* about such a philosopher-ruler being the only chance of rescuing the human race from its ills (473d). The young Dionysius was clever, but impatient of systematic instruction, and he no doubt had much else to engage his attention. Dion lost favour and was exiled, and Plato soon asked and received permission to return to Athens, where

Dion joined him at the Academy. But Dionysius was still friendly to Plato, and there was an understanding that he and Dion should come back when the climate was more propitious.

Four years later Dionysius asked Plato to return, saying that Dion could come back after a year. He professed a continuing zeal for philosophy, and supported this claim with testimonials from eminent philosophers. Plato was pressed from all sides, and in the end consented. But Dionysius was no more tractable; while giving himself airs as a philosopher, he kept Dion in exile and confiscated and sold his property. Plato escaped with some difficulty from Sicily, and wisely refused to lend any support to Dion's attempt to recover his position by force. This attempt was at first successful, but Dion was later assassinated by a supposed friend, a fellow-member of Plato's circle, Callippus (who was not the only student of Plato's to become guilty of the political murder of a fellow-alumnus). Plato, his views about politics amply confirmed, kept out of them and devoted himself to his Academy.

# 2  Plato's forebears

To understand Plato we have also to look at the most significant of the earlier thinkers who may have influenced his ideas. Whether we call them philosophers or not is unimportant; the word has wider and narrower senses. At most a few fragments of their works survive, and nearly all our information comes from much later sources; so the Presocratic philosophers, as they are generically called, have been a happy battleground for scholars. From these disputes little has emerged which can be confidently relied on as true; all we can do here is to pick up a few ideas, attributed to one or other of these great men, which, *if* they were current in Greece by Plato's time, *may* have contributed to his intellectual background. It is on the face of it unlikely that all the ideas we find in his dialogues were newly-minted; and in fact there is quite a lot of evidence that they were not. Originality in philosophy often consists not in having new thoughts, but in making clear what was not clear before.

The earliest natural philosophers, starting with the shadowy figure of Thales in sixth-century Miletus on the eastern shore of the Aegean Sea, made cosmology their main interest. But the fact that the Greek word '*kosmos*', from which 'cosmology' is derived, had also a moral significance ('good order') may make us suspect that their motive was not, any more than that of their successors including Plato, mere scientific curiosity. Plato in the *Phaedo* attributes to Anaxagoras, one of these, the view that 'it is Mind which imposes *order* on all things and disposes each of them as it is *best* for it to be' (97c).

We find in these early thinkers the beginning of the urge to reconcile the 'One' and the 'Many', which is a recurring theme throughout Greek philosophy, above all in Plato. There confronts us a multitude of phenomena in the world as it presents itself to our senses; cannot some unifying principle be found to bring order into this chaos? The early cosmologists sought to find it by claiming that everything in the world was formed out of (or perhaps even *really* consisted of) some single material (Thales suggested water). This kind of solution was later abandoned; but the problem remained of finding some coherent reality which underlay the baffling diversity of the world (the 'manifold' as Immanuel Kant was later to call it). Plato had his own solution to this problem, as we shall see – a solution which depended not on physics but on logic, metaphysics and ethics.

An important step in the direction which Plato afterwards took may have been made by Pythagoras, of Croton in southern Italy (he was born on the island of Samos, not far from Miletus, probably in 570 BC). Since nothing of his work remains, and the stories about him are all suspect, it is even more difficult than usual to sieve out his ideas from those of his later disciples, with whom Plato was acquainted. For our purposes this does not matter; for if an idea which we find developed in Plato could have come from a Pythagorean source, it is less important whether that source was the Master himself. The chief danger to be guarded against is that of supposing that some idea came from the Pythagorean school to Plato, when in fact it went from Plato to the later Pythagoreans.

We may notice at least three suggestions which Plato may have picked up from the Pythagoreans. The first was that of a tightly-organized community of like-minded thinkers who should not only rule their own life together in accordance with strict principles, but provide guidance (even governance) for the polity in which they lived. Plato's political proposals could be said to be a result of the combination of this Pythagorean idea with the Spartan model of orderly government and discipline.

If the stories about Pythagoras are to be believed, he actually for a time came near to making real the dream which Plato was later to dream in his *Republic* – the ideal of the philosopher-ruler. Even if true, it did not last; for Pythagoras had to rely on persuasion, neither having nor seeking the absolute and secure power which Plato demanded for his philosopher-kings. We are told that in about 500 BC, after Pythagoras had been in Croton for some thirty years and in a position of power for some twenty, there was a revolution; many of his followers were killed and he himself had to flee. But twenty years is a long period of stability by Greek standards, if not by Plato's.

The Pythagoreans may also have been the source of the idea,

central to Plato's thought, that mathematics, and abstract thinking generally, including logic, can provide a secure basis, not only for philosophy in the modern sense, but also for substantial theses in science and in morals. It is not certain whether either Pythagoras or Plato distinguished clearly enough between the important truth that mathematics and other abstract reasonings are a crucial ingredient in science, and the equally important error of thinking that they can by themselves establish conclusions of substance about the physical world. Aristotle accuses both, in very similar terms, of a related mistake (involving, to put it in his way, the failure to distinguish form from matter): the Pythagoreans, he says, attempt to construct bodies having physical properties like weight out of abstract geometrical or arithmetical entities like points, lines and numbers. It is arguable that in the *Timaeus*, where Plato seeks to found cosmology purely on mathematics (especially geometry), he lays himself open to this criticism.

A simpler illustration of the mistake is to be found in the *Phaedo*, where Plato slides from the logically-established truth that life and death are incompatible to the invalid substantial conclusion that the soul, being the principle of life, cannot perish (105–6). This Pythagorean mistake may have infected Plato's arguments about morality too, which sometimes seem to be conjuring substantial rabbits out of logical hats.

Thirdly, Plato became very Pythagorean in his mystical (or in a broad sense religious) approach to the soul and its place in the material world – although that was not the only source of these views, and both Plato and Pythagoras may have been influenced by ideas from the East and by the 'mystery religions' such as Orphism which spread through Greece in this period. The early Pythagoreans seem (though this has been disputed) to have been mind-body dualists; that is to say, they thought, as Plato was to think, that the soul or mind (*psȳchē*) was an entity distinct and separable from the body. This was consonant with primitive Greek thinking about the soul, as found, for example, in the earliest Greek poet Homer.

Empedocles of Acragas in Sicily, in the early fifth century, believed in the transmigration of souls, and it is possible that he got the doctrine from Pythagoras; Plato certainly makes use of it. The Platonic teaching about the soul, that before our birth it had acquaintance with objects in an eternal realm, and thus can, through mathematics leading to dialectic (philosophy), regain knowledge of them in this life, has what in ancient times passed for a Pythagorean stamp; and so does his denigration of the body and its base desires (the 'flesh' in St Paul's sense), and his consequent asceticism.

Two great philosophers, very different both from Pythagoras and from each other, but who lived at roughly the same time, also seem to have affected Plato profoundly. They took up opposite points of view on the problem of 'The One and the Many'. The first was Heraclitus, of Ephesus quite near Miletus, with whose more extreme disciple Cratylus Plato associated during his stay in Athens. Perhaps because of Cratylus, Plato treats Heraclitus as emphasising the diversity and changeability of the Many at the expense of the One; for Plato, Heraclitus is the archetypal believer in universal flux, who thinks that the utterly unstable manifold of phenomena that our senses purvey is all there is. Whether this was actually true of Heraclitus himself we shall never know; his few surviving fragments are extremely cryptic and are used by scholars to support widely varying interpretations.

Parmenides, by contrast, who was born somewhat later at Elea in southern Italy, went to the opposite extreme, denying the reality of appearances altogether. Though things in the world *seem* to be constantly changing and in motion, they logically cannot be. Parmenides' arguments (in verse) are much less clear than the more fragmentary survivals from those of his disciples Melissus and Zeno (not to be confused with Zeno the Stoic). This much is clear, however, that the fundamental premiss of the Eleatics (the name given to this group of philosophers, derived from that of Parmenides' city) was that 'Things which are not are not.' This they regarded as a logically necessary truth, which indeed it must be if there is no equivocation upon 'are not'. Unfortunately the Eleatics seem (committing the same kind of mistake as we have just noticed when discussing Pythagoras) to have meant different things by 'are not' in the subject and predicate of their premiss, taking this logical truth to establish a substantial conclusion, namely that void or empty space cannot exist; and therefore, since any movement requires an empty space for a thing to move into, that movement (and by a related argument change of other kinds) cannot take place. Zeno invented his famous paradoxes with the aim of proving the same point, that the belief in motion and change leads to logical absurdities. So the Eleatics concluded that, in spite of appearances, the universe is really solid throughout and immobile.

The work of Parmenides and his disciples represents the first thoroughgoing attempt to establish a cosmological system on the basis of rigorous logical arguments. Some may hail it as the beginning of metaphysics, others damn it as the first outbreak of metaphysical pseudo-science divorced from the observation of nature; but there is no doubt that it had immense influence. Zeno's paradoxes are still not all solved to everybody's satisfaction; and we find Plato puzzling about the difficulties raised by the Eleatics. He does this in the *Parmenides*, *Theaetetus* and *Sophist*, although by the third of these the problems have changed into ones about the alleged impossibility of making true negative statements. He shows thereby that he understands (as perhaps the Eleatics themselves did) that their origins lie in logical rather than cosmological difficulties.

In the whole of Plato's philosophy we may think of him as trying, by a more careful examination of the arguments, to find a synthesis between the Heraclitan or Cratylan view, which he accepted, that the world of appearances is a multifarious flux, and the Parmenidean doctrine that reality is one and unchanging. He found it, as we shall see, by postulating two worlds, a world of sense, always in flux, and a unified world of Ideas, not available to our senses but only to thought, which alone are fully knowable. But the two-world view itself can plausibly be attributed to Parmenides, together with the associated distinction, so important to Plato, between knowledge (which is of reality) and mere opinion (which is concerned with appearances).

One other fifth-century cosmologist must be briefly mentioned. Anaxagoras, a natural philosopher of the old school, was born in about 500 BC at Clazomenae not far from Miletus, and lived in Athens as a member of Pericles' circle. He, like Protagoras, another friend of Pericles, and like Socrates later, got into trouble for his philosophy; Anaxagoras and Protagoras escaped with exile, as Socrates could probably have done if his principles had not been so uncompromising, and as Aristotle did later when in similar trouble. We are told in Plato's *Phaedo*, in a passage I have already quoted

(97c; see p. 9), that Anaxagoras attracted Socrates' attention with his doctrine that Mind (*nous*) is the cause of all physical processes, but lost it when Socrates discovered that Anaxagoras made no *use* of Mind in explaining what happens, invoking grosser physical causes instead. But all the same he may have put into Socrates' or Plato's head (it is never certain whether the Socrates of the dialogues is the real Socrates) the idea that Mind had a place in explaining how the world works. This idea is prominent in dialogues like the *Timaeus* and the *Laws*, the second at least of which was written late in Plato's life.

It will be best to leave until Chapter 7 a discussion of the thinkers, called collectively the Sophists, against whom Plato was consciously reacting in much of his moral philosophy, and who appear, often but not always in savage caricature, in his dialogues. One of them, Protagoras, has been briefly mentioned already. They belong to the generation before Plato's; that is, they were roughly Socrates' contemporaries. Of Socrates himself (obviously by far the greatest influence on Plato's thinking) I shall say little, for the reason that his philosophy is so continuous with that of Plato that scholars have found it hard to decide which views belonged to which. We have some, but not much, independent evidence about what Socrates thought, for example from Aristophanes, Xenophon, and Aristotle. However, Aristophanes' portrayal is satirical and popular, and may have had a wider target than Socrates in particular; Xenophon was no philosopher, and therefore not in a position to understand at all deeply what was troubling Socrates; and it is not always clear, when Aristotle attributes a view to Socrates, whether he means the character in the dialogues or the historical person.

My own view, which is fairly orthodox, is that we can with some confidence attribute to Socrates a concern with the difference between opinion which merely happens to be correct and knowledge; with the search for secure definitions to turn the former into the latter; with a certain method of testing such definitions called *elenchos* or scrutiny; with the application of this method to practical decisions about how to live; with the question of whether goodness or excellence of character can be taught, and if so by what educative process; and with the possibility that excellence of character and knowledge of the truth about what was good were somehow inseparable, so that, if one could impart the knowledge, nobody who had it would willingly live badly. To all these doctrines we shall be returning.

On the other hand, I think that it is safer to attribute to Plato himself than to Socrates the cautious approach to moral education we find in the *Republic*, which insists on a thorough indoctrination in right opinions before a select few are introduced to philosophy and put on the path to knowledge; and his later doctrine about the soul, with its three parts and its communion with a world of Ideas separate from things in this world − a communion enjoyed in a former life, and, for those able to undertake philosophic study, in this. This last group of doctrines may well be based on Pythagorean ideas.

The extremely deep and difficult investigations of metaphysical and logical questions which occupy many of the later dialogues are fairly obviously the result of Plato's own perplexities; Socrates and the others who influenced him got him into these, and to some degree he got himself out of them. But their solution did not become clear before the work of Aristotle, if then; though there can be no doubt that the discussions in the Academy, in which he took part, and some of which are reflected in Plato's later dialogues, helped Aristotle on his way. But between the Socratic/early-Platonic cater-pillar and the Aristotelian butterfly there intervenes a pupal stage; just what is going on behind the opaque surface of the chrysalis represented by these dialogues, and how much of the development was due to Plato, how much to Aristotle, scholars have not yet succeeded in determining, and probably never will.

# 3  How Plato became a philosopher

When we find somebody (whether it was Plato or Socrates) troubled by certain important questions for the first time in history, it is worth asking, 'Why *then*?' We have sketched Plato's situation in history and in the history of ideas; but we have so far only hinted at reasons why he, or anybody else, should have asked just the questions he did ask. But this is not hard to understand, especially to us, whose circumstances make the same questions tormenting. Although it may seem to us that the scale and pace of change today are greater than for Plato's contemporaries, they were, subjectively speaking, just as unsettled by it.

Suppose then that we ask what led Plato to put into the mouth of Meno, at the beginning of the dialogue named after him, the question 'Can you tell me, Socrates, whether goodness (virtue, excellence) is a thing that is taught; or is it neither taught nor learnt by practice, but comes to men by nature, or in some other way?' This is the question (also raised earlier in the *Protagoras*) which the whole of Plato's moral philosophy, and thus, indirectly, his other philosophy, is attempting to answer. Although Plato certainly had the philosophical temperament, and could get interested in philosophical questions purely for their own sake, moral philosophy was what set him going, and it started as the philosophy of education.

It is clear from the rest of the *Meno* (perhaps the best dialogue for someone to read first if he wants to understand what made Plato into a philosopher) why Plato asked this question. A lot is made, as in several other dialogues, of the hit-or-miss quality of Athenian moral education: here were admirable citizens like Pericles, who wanted to do the best for their children, and taught them riding and wrestling and music, all very successfully; but to make them into good men was another matter. Somehow there did not seem to be any way of doing it that offered more than a fifty-fifty chance of success. Could there be a way? How familiar this all sounds!

As we have seen, life in the Greek cities, and especially the political life which engaged so much of their energies, was a pretty dirty game, and becoming more so. It was natural to find one of the causes of these evils in a failure of moral education: in particular, in the emergence of people into public life who were seeking their own good rather than that of the city. The mainspring of Socrates', and through him of Plato's, philosophical endeavours was the desire to diagnose the trouble and find a remedy.

The remedy that they were to propose comes out very clearly in the *Meno*. Right at the beginning, Socrates says that he cannot answer Meno's question, whether goodness (or excellence) can be taught, before he knows what it *is*. His point, brought out later, and already made in an earlier dialogue, the *Laches* (190b), is that one is bound to fumble in teaching anything unless one knows what one is trying to teach. But does anybody know this? If somebody had this knowledge, and so was able to teach men to be good men in the kind of way that riding-instructors teach them to be good horsemen or flute-teachers teach them to be good flautists, then by putting him in charge of the education of the young we should ensure a supply of good men in public life, instead of the present inferior crop.

But here Plato makes a very important distinction. It is possible to be a good man, in a manner of speaking, without *knowing* what it is to be a good man. For practical purposes, a man may lead an exemplary life on the basis of what Plato calls 'right opinion' or 'true belief'. This will lead him to do all the right things and give excellent advice to others. But this condition of unreasoned right living is an unstable one. Someone may start with all the best opinions and habits, and then something may happen to upset these (for example, his encountering new ideas propagated by some charismatic intellectual figure).

This, indeed, is exactly why the Athenians sent Socrates to his death: for 'corrupting the young'. They took him as a paradigm of the kind of 'sophist' (as these new intellectual gurus were called) who was leading the young astray. In this witch-hunt they were egged on by Aristophanes, who in his comedy *The Clouds* portrays Socrates as a sophist, turning the young away from their old good habits and putting all kinds of strange new ideas into their heads which undermined their morality; and the play ends with a powerful incitement of his audience to violence. But perhaps Socrates' attackers had got hold of the wrong man. If Plato was right, it was

Socrates who was pointing the way to a solution of the problem.

In Plato's reconstruction of Socrates' defence at his trial, he makes him, after he has dismissed Aristophanes' caricature as mixing him up with teachers of a quite different stamp, go on later to narrate a story about himself. The Delphic oracle (a highly respected and authoritative source of religious doctrine and political advice) had said of him that he was the wisest man in Greece. In his efforts to discover what could be meant by this, he had engaged in many conversations with people who were reputed to know about all kinds of things, but who revealed, through their failure to give a satisfactory account of what they claimed to know, that they did not have *knowledge* at all. We may take some of the early dialogues as Plato's versions of encounters of this kind. Socrates concluded that the reason why the oracle called him the wisest man was that he alone knew that he did not know; the others thought they knew but did not.

Near the end of the *Meno* Socrates makes a related point, that although there are few things that he knows, one of these is that there is a difference between knowledge and right opinion (98b). The difference, he says, is that knowledge of anything is 'tied down' by the ability to give a reason for what we know, and this makes it, unlike right opinion, something abiding which will not run away. This demand for a 'reckoning of the reason' or 'account of the explanation' or 'definition of the cause' or 'explicit answer to the question "Why?"' (no one translation is adequate) is Socrates' and Plato's most central and seminal idea.

If we combine this with the point made already, that it is knowledge of what goodness is that enables us to teach it, we can already see the outlines of the proposal which Plato thought he got from Socrates. What we have to do is to find a way of knowing, as opposed to merely having opinions about, what things are, and above all what goodness is. We shall then be able, if we are allowed to, to pass on a stable kind of goodness to future generations. This is the programme of the *Republic*, and there are clear anticipations of it at the very end of the *Meno*.

Let us look more closely at the elements in this programme, in order to understand the task which Plato had set himself, and some of its problems. First of all, there is the idea that the teaching of goodness is somehow like the teaching of riding or flute-playing, which means that goodness itself is some kind of attainment like these. But is it? We use the same word 'good' for a good flautist as for a good man. Does it mean the same in both cases? To answer either 'Yes' or 'No' to this question can be highly misleading, because 'mean the same' is ambiguous. But at any rate Socrates and Plato were irresistibly attracted by the analogy between virtue or good living, and the arts and skills.

Plato, at any rate, saw quite soon that there were difficulties in this assimilation. In the early dialogue called the *Lesser Hippias*, a paradoxical analogy is presented between bad living and, for example, bad wrestling (374a). The wrestler who falls intentionally is a better wrestler than the one who falls because he cannot remain upright; by analogy one should argue that the man who says an untruth intentionally is a better man than one who does it unintentionally. The general point is that, if good living is a skill, then one shows one has it by one's ability to live rightly *if one wants to*. But most of us think that goodness consists in living rightly whether one wants to or not. In the Socratic manner, the paradox is just thrown at us, not resolved; but it clearly needs unravelling.

A related difficulty is presented in the first book of the *Republic* (332–3). If good living is a skill or art, what is it the skill to do? There seems no way of specifying the skill as 'the skill to do $x$' without making it also the skill to do the opposite of $x$. Another difficulty is this: if one has skill in or knowledge of wrestling, then one is a good wrestler. But is knowledge of goodness (that which, as Plato thought, would enable one to teach it) *sufficient* to make one a good man? As it has been put, is knowledge sufficient for virtue? Socrates seems to have thought so; but few people have believed him.

Another problem Plato had to face was that of what it is to know something, a problem closely bound up with the question of what the something is that we know. His Theory of Ideas (which claims that what we know has to be an eternally existing object) is Plato's answer to this question. And along with investigations into the status of the things known, Plato had to face problems about the person who is doing the knowing and about his relation to these things. His account of the soul or mind was to become the framework which held together his entire philosophy. The division of the mind into 'faculties' or 'powers' or even 'parts' enabled him to assign different kinds of mental activity to these different parts and thus, he thought, distinguish them more clearly. The mind was important to him for another reason too: as we have seen, he followed the Pythagoreans in regarding it as a separate entity from the body – an entity which could exist apart and independently. This enabled him, he thought, to solve the problem of how we can obtain knowledge about questions (in mathematics, for example) whose answers cannot be obtained by sense-perception (what later came to be called *a priori* knowledge). His solution was that the mind obtained knowledge of the eternal Ideas before it entered into the body at birth, and only had to recollect it in this life. It also enabled him to claim that after death we are exposed to the rewards and punishments so graphically described in the 'eschatological myths' at the end of several of his dialogues.

If these problems about knowing, the things known, and the knower could be solved, Plato thought that practical philosophy, which was his predominant concern and his incentive for undertaking all the rest of his inquiries, could be put on a secure basis. If it can be established that there are things which we can know for sure, and that the chief among these is the Good, then the gaining and imparting of this knowledge will be the means whereby we can not only lead good lives ourselves, but by education enable others to do the same. There remains the problem of setting up a political framework in which this education can take place; and to this problem Plato devoted his two longest dialogues, the *Republic*, written in middle life and before his disillusion in Sicily, and the *Laws*, written as an old man, as well as great parts of others. His view was that it could be done only by giving absolute power, not only over the educative process but also over the entire machinery of government, to those who had the knowledge.

It may be helpful at this point to give the reader an overview of the scope of Plato's dialogues. Though in the case of various dialogues there is dispute about their relative dating, or even in some cases about whether Plato himself or some disciple wrote them, there is fairly general agreement that they can be divided chronologically into groups having distinctive features. First comes a group of characteristically 'Socratic' dialogues. There are the *Apology* and the

*Crito,* already mentioned, and then a group of short dialogues in which Socrates sets up puzzles, especially about particular virtues or good qualities and the relation of these to each other and to knowledge. The puzzles are not resolved in these dialogues; often they are taken up later by Plato, and many are discussed in greater depth by Aristotle.

Puzzle (*aporiā*) or paradox was a recognized method of philosophic inquiry from Zeno onwards, and still is; it can be used either, as by Zeno, to refute a theory by showing that it has unacceptable consequences, or, as most commonly by Socrates, and in modern times by Lewis Carroll, simply to set us thinking about a problem by showing to what apparently absurd results the apparently logical implications of commonly accepted notions or ways of speaking can lead. We may suppose that this method continued in use in Plato's Academy, and that many even of the later dialogues reflect it (though in them Plato is not so chary of positive conclusions); no doubt the puzzles were discussed *ad nauseam* among his students. Aristotle, a participant, produces elegant solutions of some of them. Concentrated examples of such a technique occur in the *Euthydemus,* whose combination of sophistication and *naïveté* has made it hard to date with confidence.

In this first group we may include, besides the dialogues just mentioned, the *Euthyphro, Laches, Lysis, Charmides, Theages, Greater* and *Lesser Hippias, Ion* and *Greater Alcibiades.*

Second in chronological order comes a group of longer dialogues, probably spanning the period of Plato's life immediately before and after his first visit to Sicily. This contains the *Protagoras, Meno, Gorgias, Phaedo, Symposium,* and *Phaedrus,* as well as that oddity the *Menexenus* (see p. 2). This was perhaps the most crucial phase in Plato's development; the Socratic puzzles about the virtues are discussed more deeply and connectedly; important positive and substantive doctrines are introduced concerning morality, education and politics; there are two marvellous disquisitions on love; and the 'Theory of Ideas', to be discussed in Chapter 5, makes a gradual appearance, with its insistence that to the moral and other qualities there correspond eternally existing entities, available to inspection by an instructed mind, which either are the models of such qualities, or give them to things by being present in them, or both.

Along with this development comes a strong dose of Pythagorean-ism (plausibly connected by scholars with the visit to Italy and Sicily). Plato propounds the view that our souls are immortal and had access to these Ideas in a previous existence.

The *Republic* was probably also written during this time. Since its composition may have taken many years, it is unprofitable to speculate on its dating in relation to this second group (especially the *Phaedrus*). Many scholars think that its first book, which has the characteristics of the earliest group, started life as a separate piece, and that the rest was written much later. The topic of the whole dialogue is 'uprightness' or 'right living', and whether it is to be recommended as good policy for those seeking happiness; this leads Plato into large-scale proposals on how society should be organised (see Chapter 9). It also contains the first full-dress exposition of his views about the nature of knowledge and about philosophical method.

There is no agreement about the date of the *Cratylus*, devoted to the philosophy of language; but it is plausible to put it somewhere in this middle period. The rest of the dialogues, up to Plato's last work the *Laws*, show a trend away from the use of Socrates even as a mouthpiece for Plato's views; often he gets altogether displaced from the discussions, though in the *Philebus*, contrary to this trend, he again plays the chief role. In the *Parmenides* Socrates when young encounters the distinguished Eleatic philosopher of the preceding generation and his disciple Zeno, and, defending in a rather naïve way the Platonic Theory of Ideas, receives something of a troun-cing; but he comes back with some telling criticisms of Parmenides' own system. It is natural to take this dialogue as an introduction to the series which includes the *Theaetetus*, *Sophist* and *Politicus* (or *Statesman*). In these, difficulties in the earlier Socratic or Platonic doctrines are penetratingly discussed, and an attempt is made to come to terms with the views of Protagoras, Heraclitus and above all the Eleatics. This leads Plato into very deep waters, into which we shall not be able in this little book to follow him. Plato's chosen philosophical method, called 'dialectic', is further developed, and new moves in it called 'collection' and 'division' (see p. 44) are explained and illustrated at length. The *Politicus'* main object is to expand on Plato's political theory, and it forms a kind of bridge between the *Republic* and the *Laws*.

Scholars disagree on the extent to which Plato modified, or even abandoned, his Theory of Ideas as a result of the criticisms voiced in the *Parmenides* (see p. 34). It is perhaps safest to say that he did not abandon it, but sought to preserve it by more careful exposition and restatement in other words, as he did in the case of the Socratic doctrine about the relation of knowledge to virtue. One of the bones of contention is whether the *Timaeus*, in which the Theory features in something like its earlier form, was written near the end of Plato's life, as used to be generally thought, or whether it belongs to the middle period. There are also passages in the *Politicus* (285d, e) and the *Philebus* (61d, e) which are at any rate couched in the language of the Theory.

The *Timaeus* is a work on cosmology, which has appended to it the *Critias*, an unfinished fragment about the lost island of Atlantis, the conquest of which by an earlier Athenian state governed in Plato's ideal manner was to have been the main subject of the dialogue. The town planning and administrative arrangements of Atlantis are described in engaging detail. The *Philebus*, almost certainly a late dialogue, returns to the subject of the rival merits of pleasure and thought as ingredients in the good life, and in the course of the discussion further pursues the exposition of the dialectical method and the problem of the One and the Many. Lastly the *Laws*, Plato's longest work and probably unrevised, expounds in detail his legislative proposals for his ideal state, somewhat modified from the *Republic*, in the direction (anticipated in the *Politicus*) of greater practicability.

# 4 Understanding Plato

After this necessarily brief survey of Plato's development, we are in a position to look at some of his ideas more closely. But first a warning is necessary. Anybody who takes up one of the early dialogues will have the impression that Plato is a very clear writer; and he certainly writes in a delightfully readable style. That, indeed, is one of the reasons why so many still read him. So the difficulty of really understanding him may not at first be apparent. The trouble is not so much that he writes entirely in dialogue form, so that he might not himself be meaning to endorse the views put into the mouth of one of his characters. Dialogues can be very clear; there is no difficulty, for example, in knowing what is going on in Berkeley's or Hume's. Nor is it that Socrates, the chief character in all the early dialogues, is usually unwilling to state his own views (which, we might assume, Plato would wish us to accept), and likes more to reduce those of others to absurdity. The main difficulty is one about Plato's situation in time: he comes in at the beginning of philosophy as we understand the term (what his predecessors except Socrates had been doing was not quite the same); and therefore he had to invent the method and the terminology as he went along. Not surprisingly, he did not become clear all at once, or sometimes even at all, about the issues he raised.

There is a style of interpretation, practised on Plato by many modern commentators, which goes like this. They first point to some passage in the dialogues whose meaning is not entirely clear. They then suggest various statements in modern English of what he might have meant, and draw consequences from each of them to which they think he would be committed if that were what he meant. If these consequences are absurd or inconsistent, they then, according to their temperaments, either write him off as a bad philosopher, or conclude that, since he was not a bad philosopher, he cannot have meant that.

Although the method has some resemblance to Socrates' treatment of his opponents, it is unfair in that Plato is not here to answer back, and is in any case unsound as a method of getting at what he meant.

It is far safer not to attribute to Plato any proposition which cannot be translated into Greek, the language in which he did his thinking. If it cannot be, he cannot have thought that. One is handicapped when writing a short book about Plato in English, and I shall probably find myself committing the fault I have just been condemning, but to be on secure ground, if his own words are unclear or ambiguous, the most we can do is to imagine that we have him with us, put to him questions in Greek, and then speculate as to how he might answer them in Greek. If this method is followed, it will be found that many of the distinctions on which, as modern philosophers, we rightly want to insist, pass him by.

If we want to ask what Plato *would* have said, if he had lived now and had read Hume, Kant, Carnap, Wittgenstein etc., about questions for the posing of which these distinctions are necessary, we can, if we like, imagine additionally that we can teach him modern philosophical English and speculate as to what answers he would then give; but it *will* be speculation (good philosophical training though it is for ourselves), and cannot in any case pose as an interpretation of his views as expressed in the dialogues. What we can do is to look at those views, and then at the subsequent history of philosophy, and see what, in the hands of others, they *turned into*. There are many striking affinities between what Plato said and what later thinkers have said, even some who are not called Platonists; nearly all philosophers are heavily in debt to him. We can therefore, when reading Plato, often find the seed of some later idea. But it is seldom more than a seed.

Later thinkers who acknowledge debts to Plato, or, by contrast, who have reacted against him, often attribute to him views which have been suggested to them by reading him; but this is a dangerous game. Aristotle played it (perhaps with greater right than most, because he knew Plato personally and was taught by him). So did the Neoplatonists in late antiquity, our own Cambridge Platonists in the seventeenth century, and Hegel and other romantic philosophers in the nineteenth. And so do some modern philosophers of mathematics. It is by no means clear that Plato was a 'Platonist' in any of these senses. The problem is compounded by the fact that, although his thought has a remarkable unity, there are different aspects to it which different disciples have seized on.

Let us dramatise the two most prominent of these aspects by imagining that we are speaking not of one person but of two (which is indeed what one *would* imagine, if one compared some commentators with some other commentators). I shall call these two characters Pato and Lato. Pato is an advocate of what Aldous Huxley called 'the perennial philosophy'. He believes in a total difference in kind between the spiritual and the material, the immortal soul and the perishable body, the world of eternal Ideas and 'the world of matter and of sense' as Newman called it; and he endows this difference with a moral significance. The eternal verities are also eternal values, and the soul's task in its thousand-year cyclical journeys is to strive towards these and escape from the contamination of the flesh. These thoughts make Pato into the stern and ascetic moralist portrayed in Raphael's Vatican fresco; he would have been at home in a Zen Buddhist monastery, or even in Egypt with the desert fathers.

Lato seems at first entirely different. He is interested in science, especially in mathematics, and thus in logic and the philosophy of language. He taught Aristotle, and set him on the way to becoming the world's greatest logician and a notable biologist. He has learnt from Socrates to ask searching questions like 'What is justice (or The Just)?' – questions to which the answer would be a definition – and to submit proposed answers to destructive scrutiny, using logical and conceptual and linguistic techniques which he or Socrates invented. He follows Socrates in being an exposer of intellectual pretensions which are not founded on real understanding of what one is saying; but at the same time he encourages us to believe that if we *could* understand, reason would supply us with answers to the questions that trouble us. This intellectual midwifery, the sorting out of genuine from bogus offspring of the mind, makes the name 'Lato' appropriate, because Lato was the Greek goddess of childbirth, and Socrates claims in the *Theaetetus* to have learned the art from his midwife mother (149a).

The two characters are very different; so it is not surprising that the Patonists and the Latonists have given contrasting pictures of Plato. Readers of him will always be tempted to pick out those of his ideas which they find congenial, and forget about the others. In this book I am trying not to do that; but it is very hard. One expedient which I would recommend to anyone who wants to understand Plato is this: sometimes allow him to be unclear. There are many philosophical questions which had not arisen in Plato's time. No doubt, if he were going to be absolutely clear on some issues, he would have had to give a definite answer to such questions. But he did not; and it is historically sounder not to force upon him one answer or another, but rather to leave the questions unanswered, which means leaving his doctrine indeterminate at those points. It goes without saying that Plato was capable of making very clear and precise distinctions, and often does so, for the first time in philosophy, to good effect. But he had not made all that there are to be made; that would be too much to expect of somebody who was creating a whole new branch of inquiry.

We may illustrate this point, at the cost of anticipating questions which will occupy us later, from his treatment of the Socratic search for definitions. When Socrates asked questions like 'What is justice?' or 'What is The Just?', there are at least three things which we might take him as wanting. Does he want a definition of a word or of a thing; and if of a thing, of what *kind* of thing – of something we might come across in this world, or of something which is only available to thought? Let us try constructing a little dialogue to shed light on this question, without making Plato say anything which will not go into Greek.

ENGLISH STRANGER  When Socrates says in the *Theaetetus* (147c) that mud (or clay) is earth mixed with water, is he saying what the *word* 'mud' means?

PLATO  Yes, of course. And *what* the word means, the thing mud, is what one has to be able to define if one is to show that one knows what mud is. As Socrates says, 'Do you think anybody understands the word for anything, if he doesn't know the thing, what it is?' (147b).

E.S.  But what is this mud he has to know? Is it what one gets on one's boots?

P.  How can you expect me to think that? One only gets *particular bits* of mud on one's boots, and one can touch and see them, but not know them in the sense I'm after. I am after what Mud is in

itself, not after particular bits of mud. In the *Parmenides* I made
Socrates reluctantly aware that, even with so down-to-earth a thing
as mud, there is this Mud-in-itself that one has to know if one is to
have knowledge what mud is (130c).

E.S.   So when Socrates says mud is earth mixed with water, is he
defining a word or a thing?

P.   I don't see the difference. To define the word is to say what
the thing is that it means. But this thing isn't what one gets on
one's boots; it is what the mind has before it when one thinks of
mud.

E.S.   Perhaps we could make the matter clearer if I asked you
whether Socrates' definition is the sort of thing that would go into
a dictionary. A dictionary is a collection of definitions rather like
that first one you or your students compiled and which got into
your works under the name *Definitions*. We have very big diction-
aries now; the biggest is produced in Oxford and *it* defines 'mud'
as 'a mixture of finely comminuted particles of rock with water'
(you see, we like to be more exact nowadays). Other definitions in
it which are very like those to be found in your *Definitions* are
'even: the latter part or close of the day' (cf. 411b); 'wind: air in
motion . . . usually parallel to the surface of the ground' (cf. 411c).
And you might find the following familiar: 'circle: a plane figure
. . . bounded by a . . . circumference, which is everywhere equally
distant from a point within, called the centre'; at least there is
something very like this in that famous *Seventh Letter* attributed to
you (342b).

P.   Your dictionary does sound as if it were after the same sort of
things as I am after, namely statements in words of what other
words mean; and of course what they mean are Ideas.

Without prolonging the dialogue, I think we can claim that it is
simply not profitable to ask Plato the question 'Are you defining
words or things?', because he would not understand what we were
asking. In general it is very unclear, and contentious even among
philosophers today, whether metaphysics, logic and linguistics are
separate disciplines (we would not get a straight answer from either

a logical positivist like Rudolf Carnap or an idealist like F. H. Bradley); and therefore it is not surprising that Plato cannot tell us which he is doing. But in what follows we may be able to shed a bit more light on another question, namely why he found the distinction between definitions of words and definitions of things difficult.

# 5 Knowing things

One of Plato's chief incentives to metaphysics was a nest of problems he thought he had encountered about knowledge. To understand his trouble, the first thing to get clear is, What did Plato think was the object of knowledge (that is, *what* somebody knows)? If the first of these expressions does not translate easily into Greek, the second does; and it is all right in Greek, and still quite natural in English, to say things like 'I know something.' 'Does the man who knows know something or nothing?' asks Socrates in the *Republic*; and, having got the obvious answer that he knows something, elicits the further answer that this something is an entity, an existing thing (476e).

As we shall see, Plato did not clearly distinguish between *what exists* and *what is true* (at least not in his earlier work; the distinction is at least hinted at in the *Timaeus* (29c)), and this may have been an extra source of confusion. It is easy to slip from the correct idea that what is known must be true to the mistaken idea that what is known must exist. If we speak in this way of an object of knowledge, we are implying that knowledge is some sort of relation between two things: the knower, that is the person who knows, or his mind or knowing faculty, and an object, that is the thing known, or what he knows. The relation can be thought of as like that between us (or our eyes) and a bird when we see a bird. This way of thinking about knowledge, natural though it is, can lead to a lot of trouble.

If the question 'What is this thing that we know?' is once raised, a modern philosopher is likely to answer 'The truth of a proposition' or, more simply, 'That (for example) five is a prime number', or 'That pigs can't fly.' For those of us who speak in these terms the status of the 'things known' called truths or propositions will be highly obscure, and has troubled many moderns; but it did not trouble Plato, because he did not look at the matter in this way. If he had, he would have been less tempted to (as the professionals say) 'hypostatise', or 'reify', the objects of knowledge (that is, suppose that they are existing things); for, although some philosophers have postulated entities out in the world called propositions, they take a bit of swallowing.

We may note that, even on a propositional view of knowledge, problems arise of a somewhat Platonic sort. Whenever we make a statement, it has to be *about* something (its subject). In the *Sophist* the Eleatic Stranger says 'If it weren't about anything, it wouldn't be a statement at all; for we showed that to be a statement, but one about nothing, is impossible' (263c). This true point is familiar from modern discussions. But it raises difficulties in the case of statements with abstract subjects, such as 'The circle is a plane figure, etc.' This is not a statement about any particular circle or even about any specific kind of circle; but unless we can identify what the person who makes it is talking about, how can we be sure he is talking about anything?

But Plato was not attracted by a propositional view of knowledge. This was partly because of some features of Greek idiom, which, in combination with other traps, led him to posit, as the objects of knowledge, Ideas existing in an eternal realm which are not propositions but *things*. I shall use the word 'Idea', with a capital 'I', to translate Plato's '*ideā*' and '*eidos*' (sometimes also translated 'Form'); but it must be understood that he meant by these a kind of object independent of the mind, with which the mind could become acquainted, and not anything merely mental (i.e. existing only in the mind).

The first feature of Greek idiom which may have misled Plato is this. Greek tends to put what looks like a direct object after verbs of knowing. It says, commonly though not always, 'I know *thee* who thou art'. The dialogues are full of examples of this construction. Given its possibility, it was easy for Plato to think of knowledge as a relation between a knower and a *thing*, the thing being not a proposition but rather the thing denoted by the subject of the 'that'-clause or the indirect question, as in 'I know Meno, who he is', or 'I know Meno, that he is rich' or '. . . whether he is rich'.

There are cases in which it is perfectly natural and indeed correct to use 'know' with a direct object. We can know stories, and know geometry, for example. With some other related verbs it is even easier. 'Understand', but not 'know', is used even in English in a way that could capture the meaning of Plato's Greek in some contexts, as in 'He understands justice (i.e. what it is)'; and the commonest word for 'understand' in Greek is also one of Plato's favourite words for 'know'. Since we can also speak of understanding the *word* 'just', this does something to explain Plato's difficulty, already noticed, in separating definitions of words from definitions of things.

But Plato more commonly uses a different model from these, also natural in English as in Greek: the model of what is now often called 'knowledge by acquaintance'. It is common nowadays to distinguish the kind of knowing expressed by '*savoir*', '*wissen*' and '*scire*' from that expressed by '*connaître*', '*kennen*' and '*cognoscere*' ('I know that pigs can't fly' from 'I know Meno' and 'I know Athens'). Significantly, though Greek has a word cognate with (that is, related etymologically to) the second set of verbs for knowing, it does not use it, any more than English uses 'know', to make this distinction, but allows it indiscriminately to govern direct objects, or 'that'-clauses, or both combined ('I know Meno, that he is rich'), or the equivalent participial construction ('I know Meno, being rich', as Greek puts it); and similarly the verb which is cognate with '*wissen*' is used in all these ways. It is also cognate, like '*ideā*' and '*eidos*', with the Greek and Latin words for 'see', thereby making it even easier for Plato to think of knowing as being, like some kind of mental seeing, a direct acquaintance with an object or thing. So Plato, when he wants to say something about other kinds of knowledge, often recurs to the model of knowledge by acquaintance. I have already given an example from the beginning of the *Meno*; near the end of the dialogue he does the same, illustrating the difference between knowledge and true opinion by the example of knowing the road to Larissa, as opposed to having opinions about it (71b, 97a). Plato is here setting out a theory about knowledge which is supposed to hold for all sorts of knowledge; but he illustrates it by a case of knowledge by acquaintance − acquaintance with a physical thing, namely a road.

It may have been in part this tendency of the Greek language which led Plato to posit a *thing* or *entity* such that knowledge is a relation between us and it, and to think of this entity as being somehow *like* Meno or Athens or the road to Larissa, which we know in the perfectly ordinary sense of being acquainted with them, and yet mysteriously somehow *unlike* them. It had to be unlike them, because knowledge must be of what is true, and moreover (Plato thought) reliably and abidingly true. Because the Greek word for 'true' (like the English) sometimes means 'real' (see p. 36), and because we cannot know what is false, he thought that what we know has to be real. And thinking, as he did, that we could not really know anything unless we had the right to be sure of it, the only candidates he could admit as objects of knowledge in the full sense had to be things which were not merely real, but *necessarily* real, and therefore eternal and indestructible. If we have knowledge of other things (for example, the things we see and touch) it is not of the full-blooded kind.

Plato hankered, in his search for real knowledge, after the kind of certainty which the truths of mathematics have; but because he was after things and not truths, the things had to be necessarily existing things. Looked at in this light, even the road to Larissa does not really qualify (it might be washed away, as roads in Greece sometimes are).

There are other linguistic traps too for Plato. Greek had no separate words for 'word' and 'name'. Thus it was easy for Plato to suppose that the way in which a word like 'man' got its meaning was the same as that in which a proper name like 'Meno' got its meaning – by there being an object of which it is the name (the Idea of Man). This has been called the 'Fido'–Fido theory of meaning: the view that for any word to have meaning is for there to be some entity to which it stands in the same relation as the name 'Fido' does to the dog Fido.

Another trap was the facility with which Greek formed abstract nouns by adding the definite article to the neuter adjective. We still do this (influenced by Plato) when we speak of 'The Right and the Good' (the name of a book on ethics by Sir David Ross); but it is not natural in English. It became extremely common in the political and other rhetoric of Plato's time, as can be seen by reading almost any of the speeches in Thucydides. Where we should speak of knowing what rightness is, or alternatively of what 'right' means, it is easy in Greek, because of the factors already mentioned, to speak of knowing the Right, and thus fail to distinguish between these possibly different things. And from this it is a small step to saying, as Plato was tempted into saying, that the Right which we know is a really and necessarily existing thing, which has to perfection the quality of rightness (for if the Right is not right, what is?).

This view that the Ideas themselves have the properties of which they are the Ideas is known by scholars as the doctrine of *self-predication*, or, alternatively, of *paradigmatic Ideas*. The notion of the Idea as a paradigm or ideal example of the quality in question occurs in Plato as early as the *Euthyphro* (6e), and we can see how seductive it is. And no doubt the temptation offered by this Greek way of expressing abstract nouns was reinforced by a still older way, personification. Aeschylus' avenging Furies mockingly predict that if they gave up their task, people would say 'O Right! O thrones of the Furies!' And of course the goddess Right must always be right, as the lady on top of the Courts of Justice is always just.

Plato, to his credit, came to see that self-predication leads to paradox. In the *Parmenides* (132) he presents the famous 'Third Man' argument. To simplify this a bit: if for something to be a man is for it to resemble the Idea of Man, and if for things to resemble one another is for them to share a common characteristic of which the Idea is the perfect example, then will not there have to be a third man, the Idea by resemblance to which both the first man and the second (the original Idea) are called men; and shall we not need a fourth man to account for the resemblance between these three; and so *ad infinitum*?

It is by no means clear whether this criticism, either in my simplified form or in the various different forms in which it occurs in Plato and Aristotle, is valid and unavoidable. So Plato is perhaps not to be blamed if he did not abandon his Theory of Ideas in the light of it; but all the same it *is* a mistake to suppose that for words to have meanings is (always at any rate) for there to be entities for which they stand. If we know how to use a word in speaking and thus communicating with one another, it has a meaning; and knowing how to use it is not knowing some solid chunk of eternal verity of which it is the name, but knowing the conventions for its use, and in particular what, according to these conventions, is implied by somebody who uses it in a statement. To know what 'circle' means or what a circle is is to know that if we call anything a circle we are implying that it is a plane figure of a certain sort; and in order to know this we do not have to know any celestial entities.

It is hard (for me at any rate) not to think that another factor contributed to Plato's taking this false trail. Some people have a more vivid mental imagery than others; they think more in pictures. Those who lack this gift often find it hard to understand the thought of those who have it. That Plato had it nobody could doubt who read the similes and myths which enliven his dialogues. When he speaks of 'seeing' one of these entities called Ideas, he is thinking of something very like literal seeing, only done with what he calls in the *Republic* 'the mind's eye' (533d). Elsewhere he speaks of 'grasping' Ideas. We have grown accustomed through the long use of such terms in philosophy and common parlance (along with such technical terms as 'intuition', which means, literally, 'looking') to thinking of them as very weak, threadbare metaphors; and translators often, when Plato says 'look', translate 'investigate' or 'reflect' or the like. But for Plato they were hardly metaphorical at all. Here is a passage from the *Phaedo*, keeping Plato's visual and tactual language:

> The soul, when it uses the body to look at something, by sight or hearing or some other sense ... is dragged by the body among things which never stay the same, and it itself gets lost and disturbed and tipsy, just like a drunk, from contact with such things ... But when it looks by itself, on its own, it goes in the other direction, to the pure, the eternal, the immortal, the unchanging, and, because of its affinity with them, joins their company, whenever it is by itself and can do so; it ceases its wanderings and is with them and ever unchanging like them, from contact with such things. And this condition of the soul is called wisdom. (76c, d)

It is clear from such passages, which are very common in the dialogues, that Plato thought of the difference between ordinary sight and touch on the one hand, and the mind's sight and grasp of the eternal Ideas on the other, as lying in a difference in the objects and in the organs of perception, and not in a difference in the kind of relation between knower and known. Knowledge or wisdom is a kind of mental looking − a vision of the Eternal.

But Plato did not think that *everything* which we see or grasp with our mind gives us knowledge; for believing too (in the sense of having opinions) is a mental activity of the same general kind, and opinions or beliefs can be false. The obvious account, within this framework, of false belief is to say that it is the seeing or grasping with the mind of false objects – things which 'are not'. And here the framework got Plato into great trouble, from which he may never have extracted himself completely.

The trouble arises through thinking of truth and falsity in beliefs as properties of the thing believed. Plato frequently uses the words which we translate 'true' and 'false' as if there were no difference between the sense in which we speak of a true statement and that in which we speak of a true (as opposed to forged or in general spurious) Vermeer. The spurious object of belief 'is not' what it purports to be; and Plato, because he did not initially distinguish between the 'is' which means the same as 'exists' (as in 'The British Empire is no more') and the 'is' which expresses predication (the copula, as in 'He is tall'), gets into difficulties about whether, when we have false beliefs, we are seeing or grasping or saying what 'is not', and therefore whether when we do this we have anything at all before the mind. But if we have nothing before the mind, how can we be believing anything at all? The upshot seems to be the paradoxical one that we cannot have false belief.

Plato inherited these difficulties from the Eleatics. He grapples manfully with them in the *Theaetetus* and the *Sophist*; but the beginnings of them can be seen in the *Republic*, where he says that knowledge is of what is, belief is of what is and is not, and ignorance is of what is not (477a). His conception of knowledge and belief as kinds of mental seeing of genuine or spurious objects led him inevitably into these troubles; and scholars do not agree on the extent to which he eventually got himself out of them.

It is not even clear that he always thought of belief as a kind of *mental* seeing; the 'things believed' in the *Republic* are, typically though not always, objects perceived by the senses; so perhaps he did not distinguish clearly between seeing one of these objects with the eyes and believing it (to exist). By the time of the *Republic* he is distinguishing between knowledge and belief by distinguishing between their objects (478a); but earlier, in the *Meno*, he speaks as if the same thing, the road to Larissa, could be an object either of knowledge or of belief, and finds the difference between them in the greater abidingness of knowledge, secured by a 'reckoning of the reason' for what we know (the reason being, he implies, the Idea, and the reckoning, the defining of it – 97a, see p. 41). This suggests a definition of knowledge very similar to one which has been popular, but also controversial, recently: 'true belief which has a rational ground'. Plato later in the *Theaetetus* raises difficulties against such a definition; but it is not clear whether they led him finally to abandon it (201cff.).

By positing the existence of Ideas as real abiding entities visible to the mind, and therefore qualified to be objects of knowledge in the fullest sense, Plato thought he had resolved the problem of 'The One and the Many' which had been an incentive to philosophy ever since the early cosmologists. Even if the Heracliteans were right about the sensible world – even if, that is to say, it is, considered in itself, a multifarious, unintelligible flux – still we can reason about it if we use not our senses but our minds. As he says in the *Theaetetus*, 'Knowledge lies not in the effects [of the senses] upon us, but in our reasoning about them. For it is, it seems, possible in the case of the latter to lay hold on reality and truth, but not in the case of the former' (186d). This reasoning puts us in touch with the eternal Ideas, which have each of them a unity (the one Man as contrasted with the many particular men or the many different kinds of men – it is not clear always which he means). And they also have jointly a unity among themselves, by all partaking of the Idea of the Good (see p. 44). The Ideas, therefore, have the perfect, eternal, unchanging oneness for lack of which Parmenides denied reality to the objects of sense.

Having got thus far, Plato may have been tempted to find the hallmark of knowledge in the clarity and distinctness of its objects. 'If this very thing becomes clear', he says at one point in the *Phaedo*, 'you won't look any further' (106b). If, he might have said, we can with our mind's eye discern some Idea very clearly, is not that a certificate that it exists and that we have knowledge of it? To his great credit, unlike Descartes, he resisted this temptation. He did not rely on the self-evidence of intuition. Following Socrates, he insisted that we have to establish the credentials of claims to knowledge by submitting them to a rigorous testing procedure; and to this we must now turn.

As we have seen, it was Socrates' practice to ask people who were thought to have knowledge, 'What is ...?', where the gap is to be filled by a word for something which they claimed to know about (courage, for example, in the case of the gallant soldier Laches). In Plato's early dialogues this happens constantly. What often happens after that is that the victim offers some answer, and this is then submitted to scrutiny (*elenchos*); the Greek word also means 'audit'. This frequently starts with Socrates complaining that he has been given the wrong sort of answer. Usually this is because the respondent has given one or more examples of the thing in question, instead of saying what the feature is which they all have, which makes them examples of it.

Thus in the *Meno*, where goodness is what is being inquired into, Socrates asks for 'a single form, the same in them all, in virtue of which they are goodnesses, to which someone who is answering the question, what goodness may be, can well look and point it out' (72c). The word translated 'form' is '*eidos*', which is the standard word later for Plato's Ideas; but we do not need to ask whether by this stage he is insisting, as Socrates himself probably did not, on the substantial and separate existence of the Ideas. Nor do we need to ask whether Plato has distinguished between the fault of offering *kinds* of goodness in lieu of a definition of goodness, and that of offering *particular instances* of goodness; the former interpretation suits most passages. At least we can say that Socrates is asking for some kind of definition (whether a definition of a word or of a thing, it is, as we have seen, not profitable to ask); and Aristotle gives him, rather than Plato, the credit for introducing this move.

I say 'credit'; but recently Socrates has been attacked for seeking definitions, and has even been accused of committing therein a 'Socratic Fallacy'. There are two lines of attack which must be distinguished. The first of them points out that words have a multiplicity of subtly varying uses, and that it is a mistake to suppose that there will always be some *one* common element, *the* meaning of a word ('game' for example), wherever it occurs. There may be only a 'family resemblance' between different things we call games: think, for example, of roulette, tournament chess and the game of pretending to be an aeroplane, and ask what one feature they have in common with all games which things other than games do not have.

Without going into this criticism in detail, it can be shown that it is not very damaging to Socrates' main enterprise. Granted that it may be the case that no one common element will be found, nevertheless it remains important to seek to understand what we are saying, especially when we are arguing; for if we do not understand what we are saying, we shall not know which steps in an argument are valid and which are invalid. It may be that our understanding cannot be captured in cut-and-dried definitions, a single one for each word, but that was not Socrates' or Plato's main point. They were acquainted with the phenomenon of ambiguity, and if it is more complex than they thought, it still does not diminish the importance of understanding.

The other line of attack would be more damaging if it could be sustained. '*Before* we start trying to define a word', it may be said, 'we have in some sense to know how to use it. We have *either* to be able to point to examples of its correct use, *or* to be able to explain its meaning in words. If we can do neither of these things, we cannot even start. But pointing to examples is a perfectly legitimate way of starting, and Socrates does wrong to ban it. When the word that is being asked about is a moral word, Socrates' move can be very harmful. For instance, we all know how to pick out examples of courage, but many of us find it hard to define the word. If Socrates asks us what courage is, and we cannot provide an answer which satisfies his rigorous standards, we may come to think that we don't know what it is, or wonder whether the acts we thought had it in fact had it, or even whether there is such a thing; and this may be bad for our moral characters. Socrates therefore really is corrupting the young'.

Behind this criticism lies a theory about meaning which must now be brought out into the open. The most famous modern statement of this claims that 'if language is to be a means of communication there must be agreement not only in definitions but, queer as this may sound, agreement in judgements also'. You and I cannot be using a word in the same way unless there are some uses of it which we agree to be correct, and this implies that we agree on at least some substantial and not merely verbal questions. Unless, for example, there are some things we agree to be pigs, we cannot be using the word 'pig' in the same way. This may be true of certain classes of words; but that it is true of all words has not been established. In particular, it is highly disputable in regard to value words. Is it not possible for you and me to be in radical disagreement on how one ought to behave, so that we cannot find *any* 'ought'-statement on which we could agree, and yet be using the word 'ought' in the same way? If we did not mean the same by the word, our attempts to voice our disagreements would founder; for when I said 'He ought' and you said 'He ought not', we should merely be at cross purposes.

However, it is not necessary for us to insist on this point in order to defend Socrates. For he could easily grant initially that we do have a 'right opinion', or at least a consensus, right or wrong, that such and such acts are courageous, and that this enables us to get along all right with the word; but go on, first to deny that this right opinion amounts to knowledge (it does not have the necessary certitude or abidingness), and secondly to say that what would give it this more reliable quality would be some sort of deeper under-standing of what we say. What is being challenged, in this criticism, is the Socratic-Platonic distinction between knowledge and right opinion. The basis of the attack is that right opinion (in Greek *orthē doxa*, the etymological ancestor of 'orthodoxy') ought to be enough for the upright man.

If the attack were justified, then perhaps philosophy itself ought never to have started. For what above all got philosophy started was Socrates' and Plato's insistence that right opinion is not enough; it is utterly unstable and unreliable unless it is turned into secure know-ledge by 'a reckoning of the reason'. 'A reason' is what Socrates is asking for in his 'What is . . .?' questions. If we could understand the words used in setting out the problems that trouble us, we might then go on to find secure solutions to them. That really is what philosophy is about, and so those who press this attack are revealing themselves as antiphilosophers, like the Athenians who put Socrates to death on substantially the same grounds. As a great modern philo-sopher of mathematics, Gottlob Frege, put it, echoing Socrates and speaking of people who held that definitions were unnecessary in mathematics: 'The first prerequisite for learning anything is thus utterly lacking − I mean, the knowledge that we do not know.'

In default of this deeper understanding, popular agreement is not enough, and is often (especially at times of moral uncertainty like Plato's and our own) not forthcoming. It is to be noted that Euthyphro, in a dialogue which has been singled out for attack, is in *disagreement* with the rest of his family on whether he would be doing his religious duty if he prosecuted his father for the manslaughter of a servant who had murdered another servant. If it was a real case, there was no doubt dissension about it in the city at large. In such a case there is no orthodoxy to appeal to, and we have, however much we should like the comforts of moral assurance, to think the thing out for ourselves. This is what Socrates and Plato are trying to find a way of doing, and the importance of their endeavour for the theory and practice of moral education is, as we shall see, immense.

We must now ask how Plato thought the Socratic question could be answered − what philosophical method he was proposing. As we have seen, he had rejected the mere clarity of a thought as a certificate of its correctness, and was not going to rely on general assent either. Instead, he demanded what he called 'a reckoning of the reason' for thinking it. And this was to take the form 'The . . . is —', that is, some kind of definition. This is what Plato called 'an account (*logos*) of the being' of something. The phrase was adopted by Aristotle, and is the lineal ancestor of the modern expression 'essential definition'. But it is important when reading Plato to keep in mind that it means no more than an answer to the Socratic question 'What is . . .?' Plato thought that the thing about which the question was asked was an eternally existing entity, an Idea, and that the definition was a description of this entity. It is doubtful whether Socrates thought this, and Aristotle did not. Those who follow William of Occam in thinking that such entities ought not to be multiplied more than we have to will seek to discard Plato's separately existing and eternal Ideas, while salvaging all that they can of his philosophical enterprise. This aim probably motivated Aristotle, and it is indeed remarkable how much can be salvaged.

Socrates' method of 'scrutiny' consists in eliciting from his victims answers to his questions, and then demolishing them by showing them to be inconsistent with other opinions which the victims are not willing to give up. Often these are generally accepted views. An example is the first definition of 'rightness' or 'uprightness' considered in the *Republic*: 'Truthfulness, and the giving back of anything that one receives from anybody' (331c). This is rejected because it would have the consequence that, if one had been lent some weapons by a friend, and he had gone mad, it would be right, or upright, to give them back to him.

Unfortunately there are two ways of taking this argument, which have not been generally distinguished, and were not by Plato. Is he saying that any definition which runs counter to the opinions of its proposer, or to received opinion, is to be rejected? This would invite the objection that the opinions might be wrong, and not the definition. However, Plato is generally thought to be proposing such a method of refutation.

He would be on safer ground if he were saying that any definition which can be shown to run counter to the linguistic usage of native speakers is to be rejected. The argument would then go: 'All of us would call the act of giving back the weapons to the madman "not right"; this universally held opinion, whether or not it is *correct*, is certainly not *self-contradictory*; so the definition, which makes it self-contradictory, must be wrong.' On this way of taking the argument, the method is sound by the usual canons of scientific method: a linguistic hypothesis about the meaning of a word has been advanced, and is refuted by showing that the linguistic facts do not square with it. We have already noticed the difficulty of attributing to Plato a clear distinction (if such exists) between linguistic or logical enquiries into the meanings of words and metaphysical enquiries into the things the words mean. He certainly often speaks in the latter way, and it was therefore difficult for him to distinguish, for example, between people's opinions about the nature of the *thing* called 'rightness' and their native ability to use the *word* 'right' correctly.

What is fairly clear, moreover, is that he failed, as many moderns still fail, to make a further distinction. This is the distinction between on the one hand substantial opinions about questions of morality or even of fact, and on the other questions about what rightness, etc. are (whether these latter are thought of as questions about language or about the nature of things). It is perhaps the greatest fault in Plato's way of putting the questions he was asking, as demands for accounts of the *being* of things, that it can make us confuse substantial questions with verbal ones. To revert to a previous example, there is a substantial question about mud, namely how it is, as a matter of fact, composed (a question that is answered by putting it into a centrifuge; earth and water will be the result). There is also a question, 'What is mud?', which, as we have seen, could be taken *either* for a question about the Idea of Mud *or* for one about the word 'mud'. On neither interpretation is it about the thing mud in the down-to-earth sense of what gets on one's boots or what goes into the centrifuge. But it is easy to take the question about the Idea for a more substantial question than it really is, and Plato probably did so.

In moral questions especially, it is very easy (people still constantly do it) to confuse questions about correct use of words with substantial moral questions. If we ask 'What is uprightness?' we might be asking for a definition of a word, concept or Platonic Idea, and, if so, we ought perhaps to be satisfied with the answer which Plato gives in *Republic* IV, 'Doing one's own duty' (433a). On the other hand, we might be asking for a specification of what our duty is; and in that case we should need to be given the precepts for living which Plato provides in the rest of the *Republic*. Plato was probably not as clear as he should have been about the difference between these two sorts of question. But at least he seems to have seen the need for asking both.

The Socratic method of scrutiny is further developed by Plato, who uses the name 'dialectic' for the developed form of it. It is sometimes said that Plato's method changed but that he used the name 'dialectic' for whatever method he at any one time preferred. This is an exaggeration; his method did develop, but retained a recognisable resemblance to that of Socrates. In the *Republic* he says:

> Then do you call 'a dialectician' the man who demands an account of the being of each thing? And the man who does not have that, in so far as he cannot give an account to himself and to another, to that extent will you deny that he has understanding (*nous*) of it?

... And then the same applies to the Good. A man who cannot give a determinate account of the Idea of the Good, separating it from everything else, and battling through all the scrutinies of it, being eager to scrutinise it by reference not to opinion but to its real being, and who cannot in all these scrutinies come through with his account unscathed, will you say that a man like that knows neither the Good nor any other good thing (if he gets hold somehow of some simulacrum, he gets hold of it with his opinion, not with knowledge)? (534b, c)

The relation of this to Socrates' method of scrutiny is obvious. And so is the importance of separating what you are defining from everything else, the method later to be known as 'division', which is insisted on as early as the *Euthyphro* (12d), and is indeed ascribed by Xenophon to Socrates.

In later dialogues the method is developed still further, but not in such a way as to cut it off from its Socratic ancestry, which Aristotle, who took over a lot of this from Plato, also shares. The development is chiefly in the method proposed for setting out in a systematic form the definitions which were the answers to Socrates' questions. This form came later to be called '*definitio per genus et differentiam*'; in order to say what something is, one has first to give its genus, assigning it to the class of things into which one has *collected* everything that resembles it generically, and then *divide* up the genus into species, saying what differentiates each, including the thing in question. This method has been immensely influential in biology, from Aristotle to Linnaeus and beyond. Fully worked-out examples of it are given by Plato in the *Sophist* and the *Politicus*.

Before leaving the subject of definition we must explain why the Good plays such an important part in Plato's scheme. He calls it in the *Republic* 'the greatest thing we have to learn' (505a). The reason is in essence simple, but because it was not explicitly stated in Plato's surviving works, commentators have not always understood it. The Idea of any class of things (for example men) was thought of by Plato as a perfect (that is, supremely good) specimen or paradigm of the class. This is involved in the doctrine of self-predication which has already been mentioned. To know what Man is, is not to know what it is to be any old kind of man, but rather what it is to be a good or perfect man. Similarly, to know what the Circle is, is to know what it is to be a good or perfect circle, not just any circle that a slovenly schoolmaster might draw on the blackboard.

This means that in order fully to know what it is to be a man or a circle, we have to know what it is to be a good man or a perfect circle; and thus that knowledge of the being of anything involves knowledge of the goodness or perfection of a good thing of that kind, and (Plato would have added) vice versa. Thus knowledge of the Good will comprehend knowledge of the goodnesses or perfections of every kind of thing, and thus of their specific natures. This line of thought involves two confusions. The first is between 'good man' in the sense of 'typical specimen of the class *man*', and 'good man' in the sense of 'man having the good qualities demanded in men'. A typical man is not necessarily a morally good man. The second is that of thinking that what it is to be a good man or a good circle is determined by the meaning of 'good' (by the Idea of the Good, as Plato would have put it); it is in fact determined by the standard for goodness in those two classes of thing, which, as Aristotle saw, is different in the two cases.

Aristotle, however, follows Plato in finding a very close link between the essential nature of a species of thing and the perfection of that thing, the end to which its whole development is striving (in Aristotle's terms, between the formal and the final cause). And Aristotle's notion that we can explain everything by giving its purpose goes back, through Plato, to Anaxagoras, who according to a passage in the *Phaedo* from which I have already quoted (97c) suggested that Mind orders all things as it is for the best that they should be – an idea which, according to Plato, Anaxagoras made no use of, but which Socrates took to heart. Since in the *Phaedo* explanation in terms of purpose (of what is for the best) is put alongside explanation in terms of the Ideas which make things what they are, it is natural for Plato to speak, as he does in the *Republic*, of the Good as the source of all being, and of our knowledge of it (509b).

Plato, because he thought of the objects of knowledge as things, and of our knowledge of them as a kind of mental seeing, goes on to represent the hierarchy of Ideas as a kind of quasi-physical chain with the lower items 'attached' to the Good at the top. By looking at (or grasping) this chain we can see (feel) the connections. The chain contains only Ideas; that is to say, nothing from the world of sense is admitted into it (511b, c). This was Plato's way of putting the correct point, further elaborated by Aristotle, that true, certain knowledge (by which he meant knowledge of necessary truths) cannot be had by observation of nature; it can only be of what we can show to be true by giving the required definitions.

Plato here gets near to the notion, much used by some recent philosophers but also disputed by others, of analytic truth. His most important claim in this area could be put into modern dress as the claim that the truths of logic and mathematics, and philosophical truths generally, do not rest on observation of particular things and events, but on definitions available to thought. But, as we saw, it is usually dangerous to try to put Plato into modern dress; that was not how it looked to him, because he was, he thought, talking not about *propositions* and how they are derived or known, but about things inspected with the mind's eye. Whereas for us a definition is one kind of analytically or necessarily true proposition, for him it was a description of a mentally visible and eternally true object.

# 7 Education and the good life

We saw that Plato's search for an adequate account of knowing was motivated, at least in part, by the belief that only this could discriminate right opinion about how to behave from error, and make it secure from deviance. We have now reached a point at which it can be explained more fully how he hoped to achieve this. But we must first look briefly at the educational scene in Athens. In the *Meno* he purports to record a conversation between Socrates and some others shortly before his trial, which took place when Plato was about 28; and this gives a good picture of the situation as it would have impressed itself on Plato. It is suggested that if goodness were teachable there would be teachers of it, and it is asked who these might be. Socrates, in an ironical spirit, suggests that if we are looking for *professional* teachers of goodness or excellence, we can find them in the people known as *sophists* (91b).

This word is connected with '*sophos*', commonly translated 'wise', but often better rendered as 'clever'. '*Sophos*' covers any kind of skill or dexterity, physical or intellectual, artistic or political, and is often a term of commendation – more so than its near equivalent '*deinos*', which can mean 'clever' in a neutral or even hostile sense, but literally means 'terrible' (as in the French '*enfant terrible*'). As the intellectual life of Greece blossomed there came into being a class of people who can be compared, at any rate in their effect on society, with the intellectual gurus of our own day. To these people the name 'sophists' came to be especially applied; it means that they themselves were clever, and that they could impart this cleverness, especially rhetorical skill, to young men who were prepared to pay them handsomely enough. In the *Protagoras* 'sophist' is defined as 'a master of the art of making people into clever speakers' (312d).

In popular estimation Socrates counted as a sophist, and he suffered for the supposed sins of the whole class; but he differed from them in not claiming to be able to make people clever or impart any other kind of excellence, but only to talk with them and perhaps help to birth any good notions that they might themselves bring forth; and also in not taking any money. The sophists held a variety of doctrines, and no doubt made significant contributions to the thought of that intellectually exciting period. But in one way it is not important what their doctrines were; by making young people think at all about problems to which, in the opinion of their elders, there were right answers such as ought not to be questioned, they were thought to have unsettled an entire generation. In this sense, at least, Socrates was the most sophisticated of the sophists, and by their own lights the Athenians did right to put him to death.

In the *Meno* the suggestion that the sophists can count as teachers of goodness is summarily rejected by the traditionally-minded democrat Anytus (the man principally responsible for the prosecution of Socrates). Even one of the sophists themselves, Gorgias, is quoted as saying that he cannot make men good, only clever. Instead, Anytus suggests that the right person to teach young men goodness would be any decent Athenian gentleman (like himself, we are to understand). Socrates then gives him the usual treatment, pointing out that these decent people do not seem to make much of a go of educating their own sons. The same point is made in the *Protagoras* (324d).

The traditional Greek education which a boy would get from any decent gentleman in any Greek city was probably not unlike that prescribed, in a bowdlerised form, in the earlier part of Plato's *Republic*. Plato has made important alterations: he has censored certain passages in Homer and the other poets; and the emphasis is more on the conscious formation of character and less on the learning of accomplishments like wrestling and music-making for their own sakes. But there cannot have been any radical difference in what the boys would actually have done. There would be variations from city to city: in one the mix would include more 'music' (including the performing arts as well as literature); in another more 'gymnastic' (athletics with an eye to military training). In Sparta the whole thing was highly organised as in the *Republic*; in other cities less so. But it is obvious that in the *Republic*, in his primary education, Plato is consciously taking over, with modifications, the traditional Greek education in 'music and gymnastic' such as any well-born Greek boy could expect to receive, and such as Socrates says in the *Crito* that he himself received when young (50e).

This old education did not mix very well with the new education offered by the sophists. The old education aimed primarily at training the character, the new the intellect. A person who was successfully educated in the old way at its best would have the virtues which had made Athens what she was: the virtues extolled by the 'Right Argument' in Aristophanes' *Clouds*. We must not put it too high; we have only to look again at the *Meno* and find Themistocles, who was actually a wily devil with a far from spotless reputation, being cited as a supremely good man (93b). But Themistocles was very *successful*, and commanded the Greek fleet in its most decisive victory over the Persians, and so his sins (like Nelson's) were forgiven.

The well-born, well-educated Greek was not a paragon of virtue by Christian standards. He often wanted to make a hit in politics, and do something notable for the city; at worst he was ambitious to a degree which we should condemn; he wanted to be able to entertain lavishly (Aristotle rates 'magnificence' as one of the virtues, meaning by it having the wherewithal and the aptitude for living in style); he wanted to put his opponents in their places, and even worse; and generally to have that thing which sounds so weak when translated into English, 'honour'; but not only, it must be added, for achievements which we should call honourable.

The education provided by the sophists still aimed at what was called goodness or excellence, but in a very different way. By training not the character but the intellect it aspired to enable its products to pursue just those ambitions which the traditional upbringing cultivated, but pursue them with far greater hope of success. A principal means to this was a training in rhetoric, giving an ability to persuade courts and assemblies, and thus get one's political way. The new education played on the weaknesses of the old: the old produced ambitious but fundamentally upright people; the new fostered the ambitions, and held out greater hopes of realising them, but paid less attention to uprightness. Readers who doubt this should look at the *Theages*, and see what that young man, who takes Socrates for a sophist, hopes to get from him (125–6).

There is another side to the question. Intellectual education is not a bad thing. Aristotle puts the matter very well in the course of his mature reflections on this subject. Intellectual ability, cleverness, is morally neutral; it all depends on a man's character. If his character leads him to pursue good ends, intellectual ability will enable him to achieve them more readily; if his ends are wicked, he will also more readily achieve *them*. The situation which Plato faced was one in which a new education and an old education confronted each other, not quite as opponents one of which was good and the other bad, as Aristophanes made out, but rather as two factors which actually worked together for ill but could, if reformed on lines which he was to suggest, work together for good. In the *Gorgias* a contrast is drawn between the right and the wrong kind of rhetorician, and in the *Sophist* between the right and the wrong kind of sophist. The right kind in both cases is the philosopher who, because he *knows* the Good and everything which depends on it, can really educate people instead of just pandering to their desires and ensnaring them.

The basis, therefore, of Plato's educational reforms is Socrates' distinction between knowledge and opinion. This theme runs through the whole, not only of Plato's, but of Aristotle's moral philosophy. In Plato's ideal city the scheme is that character-training should precede intellectual training. This diverges from Socrates' practice even as portrayed by Plato in such dialogues as the *Theages* and the *Charmides*; he shows Socrates having intellectually very educative conversations with young men and offering to do it on a regular basis. In the *Gorgias* Plato puts into the mouth of a critic, and does not deny (how could he?), the accusation that it was Socrates' practice to 'whisper with three or four young men in a corner' (485d); and although Aristophanes is wrong in portraying Socrates as the founder of a 'school' in any institutional sense, he is no doubt right in implying that young people were his disciples.

Plato's developed view was different; we should first implant, by entirely non-intellectual training, right opinion leading to right habits and dispositions, and only then will it be safe, at a much later age, to introduce people to philosophy, in order that they may acquire knowledge of the Good which determines which opinions are right. The only kind of intellectual training that the young get in his Republic is mathematics, a morally safe discipline. And philosophy is not for everybody, but only for those gifted people who are capable of it, and who can safely be entrusted with the running of the educational process, and indeed of the entire state. This they are to do in the light of the knowledge which they attain, in order that the society may be one in which the good life can be lived (see p. 59).

Aristotle took over this distinction between goodness of character and goodness of intellect; and he quotes Plato as saying that people should be brought up from their early years to like and dislike what they ought to like and dislike. Aristotle's view, a development of Plato's, was that if they have acquired the habit of right desire they will be able to recognise *that* such and such actions and characters are good, but they may still not know *why* they are; they will not have 'goodness in the full sense', for which the intellectual quality of wisdom (*phronēsis*) is a necessary condition.

On one point Aristotle corrects Socrates' view in the *Meno* (88c): the intellectual quality is only a necessary condition of goodness in the full sense, and not identical with it; the qualities of character are needed as well. But by the *Republic* Plato himself was implying this. Those who have the 'that' but not the 'why' are in the same position as the good men without knowledge in the *Meno*, and as those in the *Republic* who have had the primary education but have learnt no philosophy. They lack the 'reckoning of the reason' which alone can make knowledge of the Good, and therefore goodness, secure. In the Platonic state this security has to be provided by others, those who do have the knowledge.

We see then that Plato has incorporated reformed versions of both the traditional and the sophistic education into his proposed educational system. A purged system of character-formation will be succeeded, at a safe age and for sound pupils, by a development of the intellect; and each will be supervised by people who, because they know what goodness is, know what they are about, unlike both the good Athenian gentlemen and the clever sophists.

# 8 The divided mind

There is a group of doctrines, usually attributed to Socrates, in taking over which Plato encountered difficulties which caused him to modify his views, in particular his views about the mind. The most basic of these doctrines is one about the relation of the Good to desire. Not all its versions are identical. Aristotle, almost certainly endorsing Platonic views, puts it thus: 'the Good is what everything is after'. In the *Gorgias* Socrates says 'We desire the good things', and adds that whatever else we desire, we desire for the sake of these (468c). In the *Philebus* he says (in this late dialogue certainly expressing Plato's own views) 'Everything that knows [the Good] chases and pursues it, desiring to acquire and possess it' (20d). A version passed into medieval philosophy in the maxim 'Whatever is sought, is sought under the appearance of good.'

The doctrine can be given either a logical interpretation: if you are not disposed to choose something, you cannot really be thinking it the best (to think better *is* to prefer, and to prefer *is* to be disposed to choose, other things being equal); or else a psychological one, in terms of what always, by natural necessity, happens: everything as a matter of inevitable fact does choose what it thinks to be best. Plato had probably not distinguished between those interpretations, and I must confess to a doubt whether the latter, if its obscurities were removed, would turn out to be different from the former.

A related doctrine, which Plato also clung to until the end (it occurs in the *Laws*, 731c and 860d), is that, as it is commonly translated, 'Nobody willingly errs.' A translation which makes the doctrine sound self-evidently true is 'Nobody makes mistakes on purpose'; but unfortunately the *Laws* version cannot be translated in this way, since the words used mean 'Nobody willingly is not upright.' Most probably Socrates was misled by the self-evidence of the doctrine in one version into taking the more substantial version to be self-evident too.

Also related is the doctrine, already mentioned, that goodness is somehow like a craft or skill. We saw that Aristotle rightly rejected the view expressed by Socrates early in the *Meno* that goodness is the same thing as wisdom. Wisdom (which Plato equated with knowledge and with skill, two concepts which even as late as the *Politicus* he did not distinguish) is, says Aristotle, only a *necessary condition* of *goodness in the full sense*. This may also represent Plato's mature view, as we shall see.

Allied to these views is the doctrine known to scholars as 'the unity of the virtues', the view that, properly speaking, if we have any kind of goodness, we have all kinds. This might seem to follow from the premiss that wisdom and goodness or virtue are identical; for if all the virtues are identical with wisdom, they must be identical with each other. But this is too quick; courage and uprightness, for example, might each be identical with a different *kind* of wisdom, namely wisdom concerning the areas in which those virtues are exercised; and then they would not be identical with each other. Plato gives his mature views on the question in the *Laws*; virtue is one, in that it is a genus to which all virtues belong; but the species of it differ. But he still stresses the fundamental importance, for good life, education and government, of understanding the common genus (964ff.). And it is probable that he went on thinking, as Aristotle did, that one cannot have virtue *in the full sense* (cannot be, in the words of the end of the *Meno*, 'the real thing in respect of virtue') without this understanding.

But can one have the understanding without the virtue? Only, Plato came to think, if the understanding somehow failed to be in full control of us. In the *Republic* (435ff.) he gives his considered solution to the difficulty raised by the Socratic doctrine that nobody willingly errs, a doctrine which he had defended in the *Protagoras* as part of the group of doctrines we have been considering. The solution lies in thinking of the mind or soul as divided into parts which do not necessarily see eye to eye (a doctrine also found in the *Phaedrus*). For example, when people are thirsty they still may not drink, because 'there is in their soul that which bids them drink, and also something else which forbids them, and prevails over the other'. He calls the former part desire, and the latter, reason; and he adds a third part called spirit, the seat of anger, which is the natural ally of reason against desire. The good ordering of our lives which is called virtue depends on the right schooling of the two lower parts so that they obey the reason, in the same way as good government depends on the lower orders obeying wise rulers.

The way in which this partition of the mind is supposed to solve the problems raised by the Socratic doctrines is this: We can say that one part of the mind has knowledge of the Good, but may not be fully in control of the other parts. Plato had denied in the *Protagoras* that this was possible (352b). 'Self-mastery' and its opposite are, according to the *Republic*, misnomers: in the strict sense it is absurd to speak of someone being the master of himself, because then he would also be the slave of himself, and he surely cannot be both (430e), even though common parlance, and Plato himself earlier in the *Gorgias*, talks that way (491d). But it does make sense to speak of one part of him being master, or not being master, of other parts. So we can say that self-controlled people are those whose reason is in control of their desires. But not all people are in this sense self-controlled, and of those who are not it will make sense to say that they know (with their reason) the Good, but that their baser desires, which are seeking something else under the misapprehension that it is good, defeat the reason, so that bad action rather than good, vice rather than virtue, results.

Plato did not at first divide up the mind or soul in this way. In the *Phaedo*, the soul is represented as 'most like to that which is homogeneous and indissoluble' (80b); it is natural to take this as an insistence on the unity of the soul, and this unity is indeed used in the proof of immortality. The baser desires which lead us to wrongdoing are in this dialogue assigned in St Paul's fashion to the body or 'flesh'.

But even in the *Phaedo* Plato shows that he is not wholly satisfied with this way of putting the matter, and rightly. For desires are conscious states, and the soul or mind is supposed to be the seat of consciousness. A lump of flesh does not have desires: my throat does not have desires when I am thirsty; *I* have them, as part of my conscious experience. By the time he wrote the *Philebus* Plato was expressing this point very clearly (35c); he proves it from the fact that desire is of something not physically present, which therefore cannot be apprehended by the bodily senses, but only envisaged by the mind. The premiss at least of this argument is stated already in the *Symposium* (200); this is probably near in date to the *Phaedo*.

Plato had therefore, if he was to adopt the 'internal conflict' solution, to divide up the soul. But he did so with reluctance, and at the end of the *Republic* he again, when insisting on the immortality at least of the rational part of the soul, seems to be saying that it is indivisible, only we can hardly see whether it is or not because of the impurities, the mutilations and the accretions which cling to it like barnacles owing to its association with the body (611). Since both these ways of drawing up the lines of battle between the good and the evil in us are metaphors, it is perhaps not fair to Plato to insist that he decide between them.

But the solution of dividing up the self (which has continued to attract psychologists all the way to Freud) runs into more serious difficulties than this. First of all, does it leave the self enough of a unity to match our commonsense conviction that it is a single 'I' that has both the conflicting motives? If 'it is no more I, but sin that dwelleth in me', am I sinning at all? Even more seriously, what is supposed to be the role of reason (or of conscience if that is different)? Is it its function to know the Good, or to desire it? Plato is very insistent that each part of the soul, like each part of the city, has its own function; but there seem to be two different functions here.

Aristotle was aware of this difficulty, of which David Hume in the eighteenth century was to make much. Aristotle divided up the mind or soul in a somewhat Platonic but more complicated way; but he put all the motivative faculties into one part and all the cognitive and in general intellectual faculties into another; and he said of the intellect or reason that 'by itself it moves nothing; it is only when it is in pursuit of an end, and is concerned in action, that it moves anything'. Aristotle wrestled with this problem, inherited from Plato, of how the cognitive and motivative functions can somehow *combine* to produce action; he was driven a long way towards Hume's position that 'Reason is perfectly inert', while struggling, like Plato, to avoid Hume's conclusion that it 'both is and ought only to be the slave of the passions, and can never pretend to any other office than to serve and obey them'.

If Plato had been consistent in separating off the cognitive part of the mind, he would have given it no motivative function. But then, as Hume saw, it would have been totally powerless to make us do anything, except in the service of some desire which had its origin in one of the other parts of the mind. The result would be that in his effort to explain how we could be weak-willed and follow desire in despite of reason, Plato would have made it impossible for us to follow reason in despite of desire. In the *Phaedrus* he uses the simile of reason, the charioteer, controlling two horses, spirit and appetite (246, 253ff.). Even in that simile it is the horses that do the pulling; and Plato has left it unclear what, in reality, correspond to the bridle and the spur. Perhaps all that reason can do is show the horses how to get where *they* want to go.

Actually he is not fully consistent, and so escapes this conclusion. Sometimes he escapes it by making the spirit, if well conducted, the ally of reason, providing the motive force which reason, strictly understood, could not provide. More typically he gives to reason itself a motivative power, claiming, as in a passage already quoted, that merely to know the Good is automatically to be attracted by it, so that the same faculty of reason fulfils both the cognitive and the motivative roles. In the same way, in the *Politicus*, the body of the king has small strength; he manages to govern because of the under-standing *and power* of his soul or mind (259c).

Whether this is a possible solution depends on whether there could be such a thing as Plato thought the Good to be. To fulfil its dual role of object of knowledge and object of desire it would have to be such that, once discovered, it automatically excited desire. If any-body did not desire it once discovered, it would not be the same thing which he had discovered. Two people logically could not both discover this same thing, and one desire it, one not. 'We needs must love the highest when we see it' would then become a logically or metaphysically necessary truth — and that not because 'highest' is a value word, so that to call something 'the highest' is already to express love for it. For if that were so, before we thought of some-thing as the Good, we should have to be already being attracted by it; desire as well as cognition would have to be involved in the 'discovery' of it; and that is ruled out by a consistent separation of reason from motivation. Rather, the Good has to be something de-termined independently of our wills: propositions describing it have to be factually descriptive. And yet our wills have somehow to be automatically engaged in its pursuit once discovered; propositions about it have therefore to be prescriptive as well.

Whether we can follow Plato in believing in the existence of such a thing will depend on how seriously we take the objections of some modern thinkers to the existence, or even the coherence, of the notion of 'objective prescriptions' – that is to say, of propositions which can somehow at one and the same time both be objectively established as true, independently of how anybody is motivated or disposed, *and* carry a prescriptive force. Whatever side we may take in modern disputes on this issue, it is clear that Plato, in his doctrine of the Good as an eternally existing entity, beyond being but at the same time the source of being, as he says in the *Republic* (509b), did believe in something very like what is now called objective prescriptivity; but, perhaps fortunately for him, he did not have such unwieldy words with which to express it.

# 9 The authoritarian State

Given Plato's views about knowledge of the Good, and about the role of education in making possible a good life, it is easy to see how he came by his highly authoritarian political doctrines. We can become good men and lead a good life by one of two means. Either we acquire right opinions about the best way to live, or we acquire knowledge. Both, as he says in the *Meno* (98), will serve the limited purpose of living a good life; but right opinion can never be reliably imparted, and will never be secure against corrupting influences, unless somebody – either a man himself or those who teach and subsequently rule him – has not merely right opinion but knowledge: knowledge of the Ideas, which are the explanations of why things are as they are, and are also, because of the dependence of the other Ideas on the Good, explanations of how it is best that they should be. The possessors of this knowledge are the only people who can determine what kind of life is good, and thus the only people who can provide the education (even the primary education which imparts only right opinion) and the governance which are the necessary conditions of the good life.

Given these premises it seems obvious that, if the good life is to be lived in a particular society or state, its institutions will have to be framed in such a way as to further this education, and that this will come about only if those who have the knowledge are put firmly in charge of the machinery of government. Anybody who objects to Plato's authoritarian views will have to find some flaw in this argument; and the best way to understand the strengths and weaknesses of the argument is to look for the flaws. We shall see that the argument is more secure than it looks at first sight, and that to reject it involves rejecting some views which are still widely held.

Let us first look at the political institutions which Plato actually recommends, and then see what justifications he can find for their adoption. The *Republic* contains his first full-scale design for an ideal state, though it is concerned with much else besides, and is, on this as on other questions, a bit sketchy and programmatic. The citizens are to be divided into two classes, and the higher of these subdivided again into two, making three in all. They correspond to the three 'parts' into which man's mind is divided, reason, spirit and appetite; to each class those people are assigned in whom these mental characteristics respectively predominate. It is presumed that heredity will do most of the work of assignment between classes; but Plato makes a point of saying that, if there are any misfits, promotion or demotion is to take place.

The small class of rational people is to rule the state with the support of the 'spirited' or soldier class, from whom the rulers themselves, called 'guardians', are selected during the common process of education which both classes initially share. The masses in the lowest of the three classes are excluded from any part in government; their role is to obey, and to supply the community's needs by engaging in useful trades. Scholars dispute whether Plato intends them to share in the education provided for the guardians and soldiers, but his silence on the question seems to imply that he does not.

The first stage in this education, as we have seen, comprises training in the arts and in athletics with a view to the formation of good character and right opinions, firmly implanted. Intellectual education, the cultivation of the reason as a qualification for ruling, will not otherwise be safe. Mathematics, an essential preliminary to philosophy, is offered to the children but not forced on them. They are also taken as spectators to see battles, mounted on horses for their safety, so that when they come to fight they may do so bravely. By the age of thirty a select few, who have proved themselves in all the branches of the earlier education, are judged fit for the study of philosophy for five years, after which they serve in the lower offices of state, civil and military, for fifteen years. At fifty, 'the survivors, the best of them,' are 'compelled to turn their mind's eye' to the Idea of the Good, and then take their turns for what remains of their lives ordering the city, and the individual citizens, and themselves, using the Good as their model. When not thus occupied, they can indulge in the pleasures of philosophy (540).

The innovation which Plato thinks will seem most startling is that women are to share all this, both the education (including athletics) and the responsibility of government, on equal terms with men. It must be remembered that the Greeks in Plato's time engaged in athletics naked. The picture of Californian beaches which this may suggest is quickly dispelled; we learn that the sex life of all is to be strictly regulated, mating being forbidden except at special festivals and between selected partners at the discretion of the rulers, with a eugenic purpose. Children are to be held in common, as in a strict kibbutz, treating all grown-ups as equally their parents.

The life of the two higher classes is as austere as in Sparta; Plato is insistent here and elsewhere that ruling as such is a disagreeable activity, to be undertaken not for personal advantage but for the good of society as a whole. This was perhaps Plato's greatest contribution to political theory; a much commoner view was that political power is desirable not only for its own sake but also for the material advantages that the powerful can obtain. Plato, by contrast, envisages the rulers ruling unwillingly, and only for fear of being ruled by somebody worse than themselves (347c). Being neither pleasure-seeking nor ambitious, the true philosopher, alone qualified to rule through his knowledge of the Good, can leave the pursuit of material pleasures to the lower orders.

Hardly any detail is given in the *Republic* of how the government of the ideal state is actually to be carried on. In particular, the relation of the rulers to the laws remains somewhat obscure. In the *Crito*, an early work, Socrates is made to enjoin and himself exemplify a highly reverential attitude to law; although he has been unjustly condemned to death, it would be wrong for him to break the laws by fleeing into exile, because the laws could then accuse him of going back on a compact with them from which he had benefited in the past (50). Did Plato in the *Republic* intend that his rulers should have this same attitude of implicit obedience to the laws? The question is discussed and clarified in a later dialogue, the *Politicus*, to which Aristotle's discussion owes much (293ff.). In an ideal state with ideal rulers, Plato thinks, the rulers ought not themselves to be bound by the laws, but should be able to alter them *ad hoc* to fit individual cases, just as a doctor fits his treatment to the condition of each patient. Any attempt to lay down laws by which the rulers themselves were to be bound would lead to an inability to suit measures to particular cases and to a ban on all innovation however beneficial. *Provided that the ruler possesses the art of ruling,* he should be free to adapt the laws to his knowledge of the Good.

Only in inferior imitations of the ideal state, which lack rulers with this knowledge (and such are indeed hard to find), is universal obedience to the laws, even by the rulers, insisted on. Those who do not have knowledge of the Good have to be controlled by laws. This includes the lower classes even in the best of states; for them the absolute obedience commended in the *Crito* is still appropriate. The judges are to be subordinate to the government: Belloc's 'Lord Chief Justice of Liberia / And Minister of the Interior' held a combined office which would have had a counterpart in Plato's city, in which the judiciary is 'the guardian of the laws and the servant of the kingly power' (305c).

By the time Plato wrote the *Laws* his pessimism had gone further, no doubt increased by his experiences in Sicily and the lack of progress, by Platonic standards, in the politics of the Greek cities. The main speaker plays the role of a lawgiver, of a type which was in demand when new Greek colonies were founded, and to which the Academy provided some recruits, as we have seen. By his mouth Plato sets out a lengthy, elaborate and detailed set of laws, which must have appeared extremely severe and rigid even to a Greek reactionary. They are not to be departed from, although at the end there seems to be provision for amendment by the supreme Nocturnal Council in the light of the Idea of Virtue.

In this second-best city, as Plato recognises it to be (875), the rulers are 'servants of the law' (715d). But in an ideal city it would not be so. The ideals of the *Republic* remain in another respect too; although in both works great inequality of power is prescribed, the distribution of wealth, though not actually inverted as in the *Republic* so that the rulers are poorer, remains moderately egalitarian; and it does not depend on one's income-group whether one becomes a ruler, but only on one's merit as judged by the existing rulers. The philosopher-king ideal survives (711).

A modern liberal will certainly find these suggested institutions extremely repellent. Let us then ask how he might seek to undermine Plato's argument. He might, first of all, attack the more picturesque features of the Platonic metaphysics. He might dismiss as mythological the view that there is a celestial world of eternally existing Ideas, visible to the eye of the mind provided that it has been suitably schooled. The claim that only those with this superior mental vision are competent to guide others by education and firm government might thus be defeated. Unfortunately matters are not so easy for the liberal. We can show this by restating the Platonic authoritarian argument without the mythology. In order to establish it, it is not necessary for Plato to adopt a mental-vision-of-eternal-objects theory of knowledge. Of the two alternative caricatures of Plato invented in Chapter 4, Pato clearly believed in such a theory, and he was a political authoritarian. What will be more interesting to the liberal is to see whether the more modern-seeming Lato would have to have the same political views. Lato is a linguistic philosopher. Are there views about language, especially evaluative language, which can have such extreme political implications?

It would not be unfair to attribute to Lato a view about evaluative and in particular about moral language which is still widely accepted: the view that moral and other evaluative statements state objective facts about the world, which are capable of being known. This extremely respectable position is variously known as ethical objectivism, cognitivism or descriptivism – terms which do not mean the same as each other, but whose differences in meaning need not concern us here. Lato certainly believed in the 'objectivity of values'; but he could allow us, if we wanted, to dismiss as mythological the metaphysical scaffolding wherewith Pato sought to support it. It is enough for Lato to claim that, when I say that a certain way of life is good, I am claiming to state an objective fact.

If this were granted, the question then arises of how such claims are to be assessed for truth or falsity. How do we settle whether the way of life *is* good? Various sorts of objectivist give different answers to this question; but whatever method of settling these evaluative questions is proposed, the next question will be whether everybody is equally able to operate it, or whether some are better than others at determining questions about value. For if some are better than others, will not the Platonic authoritarian conclusion follow that these superior people should be given the say in all important political decisions? If what we are after is the good life, must we not leave the ordering of our lives to those who *know* what it is?

The crucial fact here, when we ask whether all are equally good at answering questions about values, is that people *differ* about such questions. This point was discussed in Plato's school, and indeed, if the *Greater Alcibiades* is a genuine work of Plato's, as it probably is, discussed by Plato himself. The same views as are there expressed are in any case implicit in the *Theaetetus* (170d), the *Phaedrus* (263a) and elsewhere. The argument is closely bound up with the analogy between the good life and arts and skills. In the *Alcibiades* Socrates is made to point out that, whereas 'the many' are all in agreement about how to speak Greek (for example, they do not disagree about how to apply the words 'stone', 'stick', 'man' and 'horse', and therefore all qualify as competent teachers of the use of these words), when it comes to assessing the merits of men or horses, or in general making value judgements, they do differ, and therefore we cannot say that they are all competent teachers about such evaluative matters. There is, rather, a select class of people who know (that is, who have the appropriate skill) and are therefore competent teachers. This conclusion is applied to questions about what is right or wrong, on which Alcibiades has pretended to instruct the Athenians in their Assembly (111).

If it is once agreed that only some, not all, people are qualified to pronounce on questions of value, then the Platonic authoritarian argument is well under way. And it seems that this argument requires only two premises: that values are objective, and that people differ about them. It looks as if the second premiss is obviously true, and as if, therefore, anybody who wishes to avoid the authoritarian conclusion will have to reject the first. Unless, that is, we take the pessimistic view that *nobody* knows the objective answers, though these do exist. Short of divine guidance, there would then be no hope of getting our politics right; but although in the *Meno* Plato rather playfully attributed to divine guidance such successes as had been achieved hitherto, he hoped for something more reliable (99c).

It is possible to think of various ways in which a liberal might seek to escape the authoritarian conclusion while remaining an objectivist. These moves rely on two distinctions, that between means and ends and that between questions of substance and questions about the meanings of words. We shall see that the first distinction does not help the liberal against Plato if he remains an objectivist, but that the second enables us to liberalise Lato, if not Pato, in a way that could conceivably have commended itself to Plato himself if, as was not the case, he had been clear about both distinctions. But it leaves him no longer an unmixed objectivist.

It might be suggested that if we distinguish between the end (the good life) and the political and other means to it, we can say that the knowledgeable élite is indeed more competent than the rest of the population to judge of means, but not of ends. Everybody is, in the last reckoning, the best judge of whether his own life has been a good one for himself; but people can be wildly mistaken about what political, social and economic arrangements are most likely to bring it about that the maximum number of people attain this satisfaction with their own lives. But if this is so, we shall maximise satisfaction by finding out (perhaps by democratic vote, or less crudely by sociological researches) what manner of lives will most satisfy various sorts of people, and then leaving it to the experts to see to it that lives of those kinds are achieved.

To this suggestion there are at least two objections. The first is that it is not likely in practice to lead to a very liberal form of government. At any rate a great many of the vexed questions in politics are questions of means, even if we differ about ends too. And secondly, in any case, questions of means and ends in politics are thoroughly tangled up with one another. To take a simple example: imagine that we are all agreed that it is a desirable end to raise the general standard of living (in the crudest material and measurable terms). It will hardly be a liberal society if, having agreed upon this end, we leave the means to it in the hands of experts. For one thing, if the experts pursue this end single-mindedly, they will find themselves doing things inimical to *other* ends which their subjects hold dear, such as personal liberty; but if they try to meet this objection by securing prior agreement to a comprehensive basket of ends, with a weighting or priority attached to each, the sheer political impracticability of such a procedure will at once become apparent. They are more likely to succeed by submitting themselves to the judgement of their subjects at the end of a given term of office, and asking for re-election if their measures have in the outcome advanced what the subjects think to have been in their interest.

Such an arrangement, however, ought not to commend itself to an objectivist liberal any more than it would to Plato. For the question about ends remains pressing. If values are objective, as both Pato and Lato think, then judgements about the ends which ought to be pursued (that is, about the character of the good life) will be objective too, and will have, on the preceding argument, to be left to experts. So the first liberal escape-route is closed.

A more promising line starts from a distinction which Pato would find difficult, but into which Lato might be coaxed if we had him with us. The question 'What is the Good?' can be taken in at least two ways. It can be taken as an inquiry into the meaning of the *word* 'good', or as an inquiry into the qualifying properties which entitle us to call a thing of a certain kind (or, as perhaps Plato would have thought, of any kind) good. Plato had not had the advantage of reading the sixth chapter of Aristotle's *Nicomachean Ethics* I, and therefore made the mistake of thinking that the qualifying properties which make things of all kinds good are the same; but it is easy to see that the properties that make a good strawberry good are not the same as those which make a good motorcycle good.

However, leaving this difficulty on one side, let us take separately, as Plato does not, the question of the meaning of the word 'good' and that of the qualifying properties which entitle us to call things good. The failure to make this distinction is the source of the view, commonly called descriptivism, which has been almost universal in moral philosophy until recently: the view that the two questions which I say have to be distinguished are really the same question. This is no place to argue that they are not the same question (that two people may mean the same by 'good' but use different qualifying properties for assessing goodness in, for example, cheeses). I shall merely assume for the sake of argument that there is a distinction, and then see how it helps with our present problem.

If the question 'What does the phrase "the good life" *mean*?' is a different question from 'What properties make a life good?', then interesting possibilities open up. We have to ask: If Socrates puts the question 'What is the good life?', which of these questions does he mean us to answer? The first question, about the meaning, looks a good candidate for handling by means of the Socratic method of scrutiny. Various definitions or explanations of the meaning will be proposed, and tested against the understanding we all have of how words are rightly used. If we can find an account of the meaning which satisfies this test, then we can proceed to use the phrase, in full awareness of its meaning and therefore its logical implications, in argument about the other question, the question about the properties which make a life good. Our achievement so far would be a philosophical one, reached by the analysis of concepts, without any assumptions of substance about what *does* constitute a good life. If Plato were simply suggesting that this is a necessary and useful contribution on the part of the philosopher, we could perhaps all agree.

But then we have to ask: What bearing will the philosophical, conceptual inquiry so far outlined have upon the answer to the second question, 'What properties make a life good?' That will depend, obviously, on what account of the meaning of 'good' has stood up to the scrutiny-test. Without launching into a survey of rival theories in moral philosophy, let us at least envisage the possibility that the successful account of the meaning of 'good' and of other such words might put into our possession certain logical weapons – certain canons of argument about the question of what kinds of life are good – which could help us settle that question. In that case, Plato's programme would have been in part vindicated. The philosopher would have made an important contribution, not merely to the question of meaning, but also to moral and political ones.

Unfortunately Plato did not bequeath to us an account of the meaning of 'good'; and his account of other moral concepts or Ideas is not sufficient for us to extract canons of moral argument. We can only speculate about what he would have said if he had given a full explanation of the concepts used in moral argument. It is fairly safe to say that the account would have included certain elements. In the first place he would have insisted on the objectivity of statements about the good life, at least in the sense that fully informed and rational people would not disagree about what it consisted in. But he would also have insisted that statements about the good life were prescriptive, in the sense that to accept that a certain way of life would be good would be already to be motivated towards pursuing it.

It is not obvious that, when 'objectivity' is taken in this minimal sense, the notion of an objective prescription (see p. 57) is incoherent, though it probably is incoherent if it is taken in the more usual sense, in which a statement is said to make an objective claim if it is factual or descriptive. Probably Plato would have claimed it in this stronger sense; but even in the weaker sense it could serve to support his political views. For if there are prescriptions on which all rational and informed people would agree, and if only a certain section of the population are rational and informed, ought we not to crown them as philosopher-kings and let them coerce and indoctrinate the others, for their own good, into obeying these prescriptions?

The conclusion could be avoided if we abandoned objectivity, if not entirely, at any rate as regards judgements made by people about *their own* good. Let us suppose that everybody is the best judge of what is good for *him*, in the sense of what most satisfies *him*. We could then avoid the most illiberal aspects of Plato's paternalism by confining the role of his rational rulers to the tasks, first of determining what outcomes would maximally reconcile the divergent interests of all their subjects, thus ensuring for them the greatest possible satisfaction, and secondly of finding the means most conducive to bringing about these outcomes. And we could allow the subjects to dismiss the rulers by popular vote if they proved unsuccessful in this role, and elect others. Given his background, it is unlikely that Plato would have agreed with this democratic solution, but it is consistent with his main philosophical views as interpreted by Lato, except that the claim that value judgements are objective has to be interpreted in a rather weak sense. Philosophy is left with a crucial role, but it is not allowed to dictate to people what they are to find good in life.

Two further points may be made, the first in Plato's favour, the second not. First, as has often been pointed out by recent writers, we are unlikely to be able to escape being ruled by a ruling class of some kind; 'the iron law of oligarchy' is fairly well established by a study of history. If there are going in any case to be relatively few people who have the power of government and exercise its functions, even in a democracy, then Plato is surely entirely right in holding that it will be best if they receive, before they attain this position of power, an education which will enable them to exercise it wisely. Though Pato may be wrong in requiring a deep study of the eternal verities and values, Lato is on safer ground when he asks that they acquire an understanding of the language they use when they debate the crucial moral and other evaluative questions that confront the statesman. For if they do not understand the questions they are asking, they will hardly be able to answer them rationally. If Lato were to claim that this is all the education that is necessary for rulers, he would be going too far, for they need other qualifications besides philosophy. But in fact even in the *Republic* this claim is not made – only that such understanding is a supremely important part of the equipment of a ruler.

Secondly, we must make more allowance than perhaps Plato does for human fallibility. Even if we grant him that there is a skill of ruling which could in theory equip its possessor to make all the right decisions, it may be a skill which no human being will ever attain, and perhaps a skill by the exercise of which he will be corrupted. Plato is in fact fairly pessimistic about this, as can be seen by reading between the lines of the *Republic*, and by looking at the much less ambitious demands made of his rulers in the *Laws*. But Plato does not recognise, as he should, that if rulers are fallible their claim to absolute power is less strong. As Sir Karl Popper rightly insisted, it may be more important to have institutional means of limiting the harm that unwise rulers can do, and removing them without violence if they fail to secure the good of their subjects.

# 10 Plato's achievement

If the first of Europe's philosophers whose works survive does not have the same towering dominance as its first poet, Homer, that is not any reflection on Plato's genius. His actual achievement in his own field was as great. It is merely that we know a little more about what went before. Despite this, he, like Homer, presents to us the appearance (albeit a misleading one) of arising out of nothing, and also of a certain primitiveness which his marvellously polished style does not altogether conceal. He has a greater claim than anybody else to be called the founder of philosophy as we know it. But what, exactly, did he found? The answer will depend on who 'we' are; it will be different for Patonists and Latonists, and even that crude division does not do justice to the complexity of Plato's make-up, and of his influence on the subsequent history of philosophy.

Of the two Platos that we distinguished, it is difficult to think that the achievement of Pato was as great as that of Lato. The 'perennial philosophy' is perennial just because it is a very natural expression of human thinking about the mind and about values; it has appeared in many places at many times in different forms, and Plato's mind-body dualism, with its associated belief in the immortality of the soul, and his particular treatment of the objectivity of values, are not markedly different from anybody else's. What is unique in him is the progress from these quasi-religious speculations, which could have remained, as they have in others, vapid and evanescent, towards a much tougher, more precise logical and metaphysical theory, a moral philosophy and a philosophy of language; these were not entirely new, but, through discussion and criticism of them, they engendered the lasting achievements of Aristotle in those fields, and thus shaped the entire future of philosophy.

Let us start with Plato's development of the topic of 'The One and the Many'. We have seen how the early cosmologists sought an explanation of the bewildering variety of things in the world by seeking for them some common ground or reason. The search started with the question, 'What were their origins?'; went on to the question 'What are they all made of?'; but then divided. Natural scientists went on asking this second question in ever subtler forms and have been answering it ever since. But by this time problems had arisen which could not be answered by this method, and which demanded an entirely different sort of inquiry, whether we style it metaphysics or logic. For the puzzles generated by Parmenides could not be solved without asking 'What are they all?' in a quite different sense. This new inquiry, whether we call it conceptual or logical or even linguistic, consists in asking about the meanings of the words we use, or, to put it in a way more congenial to Plato, about the natures (in a quite different sense from the physical) of the things we are talking about. The Many are to be understood, not by seeking their physical constituents, nor even the efficient causes of their motions and changes, but by isolating and understanding the Idea to which we are referring when we use a certain word. This is to know in the deepest sense what it *is* to be a thing of a certain kind.

Plato had grasped the truth that conceptual understanding is different from natural science, and just as important. He had succeeded in distinguishing from each other the four different types of explanation (the four different kinds of 'Why?'-questions and their answers) which were duly classified by Aristotle in his doctrine of the 'four causes'. Of these we have just mentioned three:

1 The *material* cause, or explanation of the material constitution of a thing;

2 The *efficient* cause, or cause in the narrower modern sense, which made a thing do what it did;

3 The *formal* cause, or explanation of its form – of what it is to be that kind of thing;

and he also, as we shall see in a moment, distinguished

4 The *final* cause, or explanation of the purpose for which something comes to be as it is.

Plato was more interested in formal and final causes than in the other two kinds, and thought that they would both be understood by getting to know the Idea of the kind of thing in question. This association of the formal and final causes (having its origin in Plato's doctrine about the Good, already discussed) may have been a mistake; but, if so, it was a very momentous one which was taken over by Aristotle and by many philosophers to this day. The notion that what it *is to be* a thing of a certain kind (its essence) is logically tied to what a thing of that kind *ought to be* (its purpose) still has its adherents.

To have distinguished the four kinds of explanation would have been achievement enough, but Plato went further. He saw that there was a question about how we could claim to *know* the answers to the formal and final 'Why?'-questions. We may concede that in his theory of knowledge knowing is treated too much like mental seeing, and the objects of knowledge too much like objects of ordinary vision, being different from them only in being seen by the mind and not the eyes, and in having a perfection and abidingness which the objects of ordinary vision do not have. But nevertheless the Theory of Ideas does represent Plato's way of stating some very important discoveries.

The first of these is that the sort of knowledge we are after both in science and in mathematics and logic is something universal. A causal law or a mathematical or logical theorem, if it holds at all, holds for all similar cases. That moral principles too have to be universal is a feature of them whose importance has to be acknowledged even by those who do not follow Plato in his cognitivism – do not, that is, allow themselves to speak of moral *knowledge*.

The second is that all these disciplines including morality are capable of being structured into systems in which more general concepts or statements form the grounds of more specific ones. For both Plato and Aristotle this truth was expressed in their doctrine that in order to say what a thing is, we have to say to what genus it belongs, and then to say how it is differentiated from the other kinds of things in that genus. This is summed up in the Platonic method of dialectic, employing 'collection' and 'division' (see p. 44). We must never forget that the word Plato used for his Ideas, '*eidos*', is the same word, and with very much the same meaning, as we translate 'species' when we meet it in Aristotle's logic. Plato's description in the *Republic* (511) of the way in which the Ideas are subordinated to one another in a hierarchy may sound too crudely physical to us (it is almost as if he were looking with his mind's eye at a lot of quasi-visible onions strung together in a rope); but this was his way of putting the thought that a discipline has to be logically ordered if its propositions are to be *connected* (the metaphor survives) with each other.

In this and other ways Plato's investigations of the Socratic 'What is . . .?' questions led him a very long way into the disciplines of logic and metaphysics. Aristotle's systematisation of logic – above all his theory of the syllogism which dominated logic for many centuries – could never have been achieved without Plato's insights.

Plato also, as we have seen, avoided a trap into which he might easily have fallen, given his assimilation of knowing to mental seeing: that of thinking, as Descartes seems to have thought, that the clarity and distinctness of the vision was a certificate of its correctness. Instead, by recognising the difference between knowledge and right opinion, he was led to demand, as a qualification for knowledge, the ability to give and defend a reason or explanation for the thing known. This explanation normally took the form of a definition (ideally of the type just described). However, the importance of this distinction transcends Plato's particular theory of definition. Whenever anybody, whether in science or mathematics or moral philosophy, makes some statement on the basis of mere intuition, hoping that we will share the intuition and therefore agree with it, he should be disciplined by means of the Socratic-Platonic demand that he 'give an account' of what he has said. Even now too many philosophical frauds are unwilling to face the auditors in this way.

So far we have not, in this chapter, made much of any distinction between on the one hand science and mathematics, and on the other morals and politics. This is in accordance with Plato's practice; he thinks that all are subject to the same disciplines and methods, although in the application of them to this imperfect world rigour may be lost. But those who now wish to make a sharp distinction between evaluative and factual propositions, and thus between the methods appropriate to morality and science, do not have to part company with Plato completely even here. For one of the most remarkable things about him is how, even though he never wavered in his objectivism, and constantly assimilated moral to other kinds of knowledge, he also recognised quite early, following Socrates, the special feature of value judgements which distinguishes them from factual ones, their prescriptivity. This comes out above all in his equation of thinking something good with desiring and therefore being disposed to choose it, and thus in his acceptance, albeit in a modified form, of the links between knowledge and goodness which had led Socrates into paradox.

Nor did the prescriptivity of value judgements die with Plato. It is implicit in Aristotle's statement that the Good is what everything is after; and also in his doctrine known as the 'practical syllogism'. The conclusion of a piece of practical reasoning, he saw, can be an action just because its premisses contain a value judgement which is prescriptive. He insists that practical wisdom, our guide in matters of evaluation and action, is 'epitactic' (meaning 'prescriptive') – a word he takes over, with the distinction it implies between active prescription and mere passive judgement, from Plato's *Politicus* (260b). The same intimate connection between value judgements and action became important again in the eighteenth century with the work of Hume, who found in it an obstacle to the founding of morality on reason, and of Kant, who thought he had surmounted the obstacle; and it is still important today.

Plato was also the first person in history to attempt a systematic account of the structure of the mind. His account is no doubt crude compared with Aristotle's, let alone with what a satisfactory explanation of 'mental' phenomena would require. And he did not see the necessity for saying precisely what, in more literal terms, the metaphor of 'parts of the mind' really means. All the same, he started a very important and fruitful line of inquiry, and had much more excuse for his crude partition of the mind than some recent thinkers like Freud. Although it is hard to take seriously, as constituents of 'the mind', entities like 'the intellect' and 'the will' (to use modern descendants of Plato's terms), the distinctions which have been made in this kind of way do nevertheless need making.

They need making, above all, in order to emphasise the importance of disciplined thought, if we are to have a satisfactory way of answering any of the more difficult questions that face us. Although we have to allow credit to Plato's predecessors, and especially to the Sophists, for bringing into emphasis the intellectual side of man's nature, we owe to Plato and Socrates more than to anybody else the idea, which has been current ever since, that man will have more success in almost everything he undertakes if he learns to *think* better.

This brings us to what, I am sure, Plato himself thought of as his most important practical contribution: his educational theory. He believed firmly that there could be a body of knowledge or understanding whose attainment and handing down would make possible the orderly solution of political problems such as had brought Athens and all Greece into chaos. In this he taught the world a valuable lesson. If we could fully understand the problems, which involves understanding first of all the words in terms of which they are posed, and then (even harder) understanding the situations and the people that generate them, we should be on a way to their solution. This, at any rate, is a more hopeful line than attributing them to human wickedness which can never be eradicated. Even the wicked can be coped with if we understand what makes them do what they do. Socrates did not think he had attained this understanding, and even Plato was not all that optimistic; but he saw it as the only way out of the troubles of Greece, and founded an institution, the Academy, which he thought would help towards attaining it.

His bolder plans for political reform are more questionable, and more tentative. If the education of the intellect, preceded by a thorough schooling of the will, is necessary in order to put human society to rights, how can this come about? Plato here took a short cut. If absolute power could come into the hands of good and wise men, would not that do the trick? We have seen how much of good sense can be extracted from this bold suggestion. It is not wholly devoid of merit, but simply ignores the difficulty (indeed the practical impossibility) of finding suitable incumbents, and the further difficulty of reconciling absolute power, however wise its possessor, with the attainment of ends which nearly everybody (and who shall say they are wrong?) will include in their requirements for the good life, above all liberty. When Plato, impressed with the practical difficulties, goes on in the *Laws* to subject human and fallible rulers to a rigid code, he only makes matters worse. In its final form the Platonic proposal shares many features with the Holy Inquisition.

Nevertheless, Plato's political theory presents the liberal with a challenge which he has to face, and in facing which he will find himself having to answer questions which too many liberals ignore. If some ways of organising society are better than others, in the sense that they do better for the people who live in the society, even on their own reckoning; and if some politicians and others are doing their very best to prevent it being organised, or kept organised, in these better ways, what am I to do about them, if not seek the power to frustrate their malign endeavours? If I think I know how a wise dictator would arrange things, ought I not to try to become a wise dictator? Plato has his answer to this question; what is the answer of the liberals?

Plato did not see his political proposals realised, nor perhaps did he expect to. His only excursion into politics, in Sicily, was a disaster. But a change did come over men's minds as a result of his thought. Greek political morality did not improve, it is true; nor was the Roman much better. But though the practice of politics remained as dirty as before, it is fair to claim that, gradually, through the work of Plato and his successors, the Stoics, Christians and others, ideals of a new and better sort came in the end to be current.

The rhetoric of present-day politics is still mostly nothing but rhetoric; but rhetoric does influence people (even its authors), and cause things to happen which otherwise would not. Our political rhetoric is permeated now by ideals which were simply non-existent in the rhetoric of Plato's day. This can be seen by comparing almost any political speech nowadays with almost any speech reported from the fifth and fourth centuries BC. Politicians do not always do what they commend in their speeches; but sometimes they do, and that has made a difference to the world. Part of this difference we owe to Plato. In the end he made many people see that personal or even national ambition and success are not the most important things in life, and that the good of other people is a worthier aim. For this we can forgive him for being also the father of political paternalism and absolutism.

# Further reading *and* References

Readers who want to study what others have said about Plato will find nearly all the bibliographical information and guidance that they need in the fourth and fifth volumes of W. K. C. Guthrie's *A History of Greek Philosophy* (1962–78), which is also itself both helpful and readable, though enormously long. My own debt to it will be obvious. The earlier volumes, especially that on Socrates, are useful for Plato's predecessors. Those whose taste is for philosophically more sophisticated books might well try I. M. Crombie's *An Examination of Plato's Doctrines* (1962) or J. C. B. Gosling's *Plato* (1973) in the 'Arguments of the Philosophers' series. J. Barnes's *The Presocratics* (1969) in the same series is also good. Sir Karl Popper's *The Open Society and its Enemies* vol. 1 (1945) and Gilbert Ryle's *Plato's Progress* (1966) are two highly readable but also highly controversial books, the first on Plato's politics, the second on his philosophical development. There are a number of good multi-author volumes of essays, among them *New Essays on Plato and Aristotle* (ed. R. Bambrough, 1965), *Studies in Plato's Metaphysics* (ed. R. E. Allen, 1965) and *Plato* (ed. G. Vlastos, 1971). The latter's own *Platonic Studies* (1973) are also to be commended.

All these books are written mainly for specialists. The general reader is better advised to stick to Plato; and for this purpose there is a number of series of translations of single dialogues, some with excellent introductions, and a convenient omnibus volume of all the dialogues (*Plato*, ed. E. Hamilton and H. Cairns, 1961). More advanced, but very useful, are the volumes of translations with commentary in the Clarendon Plato series. However, accurate translation of Plato's Greek is often difficult, and nobody who bases his interpretations on translations, rather than the Greek text, can claim authority.

All references in this book to Plato are to the pages of Stephanus' edition as printed in the margin of the standard Oxford Classical Text of Plato (ed. J. Burnet, 1900–7) and of nearly all translations. In the references below the figures on the left refer to pages of this book. References to Aristotle are to the pages, columns and lines of Bekker's edition, also followed by most modern editions and translations.

Page

1 Thucydides II 35.

3 *The Polity of the Athenians* is wrongly attributed to Xenophon and printed with his works.

4 Herodotus III 38.

5 Thucydides III 82. For persuasive definition see C. L. Stevenson, *Ethics and Language* (1944), ch. 9.

11 Aristotle, *On the Heavens,* 299–300.

12 Heraclitus and Cratylus are discussed by Plato in *Theaetetus* (esp. 179ff.) and *Cratylus* (esp. 439ff.).

14 Aristophanes, *The Clouds.* Xenophon, esp. *Memoirs of Socrates.* Aristotle, esp. *Metaphysics* 987b1, 1078b17, *Eudemian Ethics* 1216b2, *Nicomachean Ethics* 1144b18ff. 1145b23ff. For Socrates' moral influence see Lysias' speech against Aeschines his disciple, fragment xxxviii in Budé edition (ed. Gernet and Bizos, 1955).

20 On Recollection see my 'Philosophical Discoveries', *Mind* 69 (1960), §viii, repr. in *Plato's Meno,* ed. Sesonske and Fleming (1965), *The Linguistic Turn,* ed. R. Rorty (1967), and my *Essays on Philosophical Method* (1971).

21 Lewis Carroll's philosophical use of paradox is delightfully illustrated in P. L. Heath, *The Philosopher's Alice* (1974).

26 J. H. Newman, *The Dream of Gerontius* (1868).

30 On this chapter, see M. Furth, 'Elements of Eleatic Ontology', *Journal of History of Philosophy* 6 (1968), and my own 'A Question about Plato's Theory of Ideas', in my *Essays on Philosophical Method* (1971) (also in *The Critical Approach,* ed. M. Bunge, 1964).

33 For 'Fido' see G. Ryle in *British Philosophy in the Mid-Century,* ed. C. A. Mace (1957).

38 Both sorts of attackers appeal to L. Wittgenstein, *Philosophical Investigations* (1953), esp. §66ff., 242. For the first attack, see J. R. Bambrough, 'Universals and Family Resemblances', *Aristotelian Society Proceedings* 61 (1960/1).

39 For the second attack, see M. Nussbaum, 'Aristophanes and Socrates on Learning Practical Wisdom', *Yale Classical Studies* 26 (1980), and P. T. Geach, 'Plato's *Euthyphro*', *Monist* 50 (1966), repr. in his *Logic Matters* (1972).

39 Wittgenstein, *Philosophical Investigations,* §242.

40 G. Frege, *Foundations of Arithmetic,* trans. J. L. Austin (1959), p. iii.

41 Aristotle, e.g. Categories 1a2.

42 On the two ways of taking the argument, see my 'The Argument from Received Opinion' in my *Essays on Philosophical Method,* pp. 117ff.

44 On the Good, see my 'Plato and the Mathematicians', op.cit. pp. 94–6, repr. from *New Essays on Plato and Aristotle,* ed. R. Bambrough (1965).

47 On this chapter, see my 'Platonism in Moral Education: Two Varieties', *Monist* 58 (1974).

51 Plato in Aristotle, *Nicomachean Ethics* 1104b11.

52 Aristotle, *Nicomachean Ethics* 1094a3, 1172b14.

53 Aristotle, ibid. 1144b17–32.

55 The biblical quotation is from St Paul, *Epistle to the Romans,* ch. vii.

55 D. Hume, *A Treatise of Human Nature* (1739), III I i; II 3 iii.

57 On 'objective prescriptivity' see J. L. Mackie, *Ethics: Inventing Right and Wrong* (1977), ch. 1, commented on in my *Moral Thinking* (1981), pp. 78–86.

61 H. Belloc, *The Modern Traveller* (1898).

65 I have tried to sort out the distinction between the meaning of moral words and the criteria for their application in my *The Language of Morals* (1952), esp. chs 6ff.; see also my *Freedom and Reason* (1963), ch. 2.

68 K. R. Popper, *The Open Society and its Enemies,* vol. 1, esp. ch. 7.

# Index

OXFORD

## MORE OXFORD PAPERBACKS

This book is just one of nearly 1000 Oxford Paperbacks currently in print. If you would like details of other Oxford Paperbacks, including titles in the World's Classics, Oxford Reference, Oxford Books, OPUS, Past Masters, Oxford Authors, and Oxford Shakespeare series, please write to:

**UK and Europe**: Oxford Paperbacks Publicity Manager, Arts and Reference Publicity Department, Oxford University Press, Walton Street, Oxford OX2 6DP.

Customers in UK and Europe will find Oxford Paperbacks available in all good bookshops. But in case of difficulty please send orders to the Cash-with-Order Department, Oxford University Press Distribution Services, Saxon Way West, Corby, Northants NN18 9ES. Tel: 01536 741519; Fax: 01536 746337. Please send a cheque for the total cost of the books, plus £1.75 postage and packing for orders under £20; £2.75 for orders over £20. Customers outside the UK should add 10% of the cost of the books for postage and packing.

**USA**: Oxford Paperbacks Marketing Manager, Oxford University Press, Inc., 200 Madison Avenue, New York, N.Y. 10016.

**Canada**: Trade Department, Oxford University Press, 70 Wynford Drive, Don Mills, Ontario M3C 1J9.

**Australia**: Trade Marketing Manager, Oxford University Press, G.P.O. Box 2784Y, Melbourne 3001, Victoria.

**South Africa**: Oxford University Press, P.O. Box 1141, Cape Town 8000.

## PAST MASTERS

A wide range of unique, short, clear introductions to the lives and work of the world's most influential thinkers. Written by experts, they cover the history of ideas from Aristotle to Wittgenstein. Readers need no previous knowledge of the subject, so they are ideal for students and general readers alike.

Each book takes as its main focus the thought and work of its subject. There is a short section on the life and a final chapter on the legacy and influence of the thinker. A section of further reading helps in further research.

The series continues to grow, and future Past Masters will include **Owen Gingerich** on *Copernicus*, **R G Frey** on *Joseph Butler*, **Bhiku Parekh** on *Gandhi*, **Christopher Taylor** on *Socrates*, **Michael Inwood** on *Heidegger*, and **Peter Ghosh** on *Weber*.

KEYNES

*Robert Skidelsky*

John Maynard Keynes is a central thinker of the twentieth century. This is the only available short introduction to his life and work.

Keynes's doctrines continue to inspire strong feelings in admirers and detractors alike. This short, engaging study of his life and thought explores the many positive and negative stereotypes and also examines the quality of Keynes's mind, his cultural and social milieu, his ethical and practical philosophy, and his monetary thought. Recent scholarship has significantly altered the treatment and assessment of Keynes's contribution to twentieth-century economic thinking, and the current state of the debate initiated by the Keynesian revolution is discussed in a final chapter on its legacy.

## *PAST*
## MASTERS

### RUSSELL

*A. C. Grayling*

Bertrand Russell (1872–1970) is one of the most famous and important philosophers of the twentieth century. In this account of his life and work A. C. Grayling introduces both his technical contributions to logic and philosophy, and his wide-ranging views on education, politics, war, and sexual morality. Russell is credited with being one of the prime movers of Analytic Philosophy, and with having played a part in the revolution in social attitudes witnessed throughout the twentieth-century world. This introduction gives a clear survey of Russell's achievements across their whole range.

# OPUS

## TWENTIETH-CENTURY FRENCH PHILOSOPHY

### *Eric Matthews*

This book gives a chronological survey of the works of the major French philosophers of the twentieth century.

Eric Matthews offers various explanations for the enduring importance of philosophy in French intellectual life and traces the developments which French philosophy has taken in the twentieth century from its roots in the thought of Descartes, with examinations of key figures such as Bergson, Sartre, Marcel, Merleau-Ponty, Foucault, and Derrida, and the recent French Feminists.

'*Twentieth-Century French Philosophy* is a clear, yet critical introduction to contemporary French Philosophy. . . . The undergraduate or other reader who comes to the area for the first time will gain a definite sense of an intellectual movement with its own questions and answers and its own rigour . . . not least of the book's virtues is its clarity.'
*Garrett Barden*
Author of *After Principles*

OXFORD

# RETHINKING LIFE AND DEATH

## THE COLLAPSE OF OUR TRADITIONAL ETHICS

*Peter Singer*

*A victim of the Hillsborough Disaster in 1989, Anthony Bland lay in hospital in a coma being fed liquid food by a pump, via a tube passing through his nose and into his stomach. On 4 February 1993 Britain's highest court ruled that doctors attending him could lawfully act to end his life.*

Our traditional ways of thinking about life and death are collapsing. In a world of respirators and embryos stored for years in liquid nitrogen, we can no longer take the sanctity of human life as the cornerstone of our ethical outlook.

In this controversial book Peter Singer argues that we cannot deal with the crucial issues of death, abortion, euthanasia and the rights of nonhuman animals unless we sweep away the old ethic and build something new in its place.

Singer outlines a new set of commandments, based on compassion and commonsense, for the decisions everyone must make about life and death.